CONTENTS

Free group Shepherding Resources available at
www.wphresources.com/joyrevealed

JOY
REVEALED

A DEVOTIONAL STUDY IN PHILIPPIANS

ALLEN SATTERLEE

wesleyan
PUBLISHING HOUSE
wphstore.com
Indianapolis, Indiana

CREST BOOKS

Copyright © 2017 by The Salvation Army National Corporation
Published by Wesleyan Publishing House
Indianapolis, Indiana 46250
Printed in the United States of America
ISBN: 978-1-63257-208-0
ISBN (e-book): 978-1-63257-209-7

INTRODUCTION
THE SETTING OF PHILIPPIANS

Philippi was founded around 360 BC by colonists from the Greek island of Thasos. Originally called Credides, it is in eastern Macedonia, about ten miles inland from the Aegean Sea.

Naming it after himself, Philip II of Macedon conquered the city in 356 BC because of its proximity to gold mines.

Because it was located on a strategic route that crossed from east to west, Philip established a garrison, built up its fortifications, added an acropolis, and increased its population by bringing in additional colonists. Philippi prospered from its location on a major agricultural plain, the gold mines, and the trading route.

When the Roman Empire conquered Greece, Philippi rose in prominence. It was the scene of two key battles. The first occurred in 46 BC when Mark Antony and Octavian (later Caesar Augustus) defeated the forces of Brutus and Cassius in the civil war that followed Julius Caesar's assassination. Routing their enemy, the victors celebrated by making Philippi a Roman colony. The residents were granted all the rights and privileges usually reserved for cities in Italy.

In 30 BC, Octavian defeated the forces of Antony and Cleopatra in a naval battle just off the Philippian coast. Octavian evicted the soldiers from Italy who had supported Antony, settling some of them in Philippi and further Romanizing the city.

The trade route that was improved under Philip was further upgraded by the Romans and made part of the *Via Egnatia*, the main road between Asia and Rome. The population swelled to 15,000 inhabitants, considered in ancient times to be a major city.

The residents of Philippi were fiercely loyal to Rome, their city being considered an extension of the imperial city.

For any traveler, it was as if one were in both Greece and Rome simultaneously.

CHRISTIANITY IN PHILIPPI

As recounted in Acts 16, Paul founded the church in Philippi during his second missionary journey, after he had a vision of a man from Macedonia urging him to bring the gospel to Europe (vv. 6–10). Paul's point of entry into Europe was Philippi, a wise choice because of its strategic location and because of his status as a Roman citizen.

The first significant event was the conversion of Lydia, a merchant of highly valued purple cloth. Lydia, along with other women who were at the river where Paul and Silas first preached, accepted Christ. She invited the evangelists to stay at her house while in the city (vv. 13–15).

As Paul and Silas continued their ministry, they found themselves followed by a slave girl whom her owners used for fortune-telling. Possessed by an evil spirit, she followed Paul and Silas around. When they finally grew weary of her constant shouting, they cast the demon out. With that, the girl lost her gift of fortune-telling, much to the dismay of her owners. That was the beginning of trouble for the men (vv. 16–21) as the owners stirred up trouble against them, ultimately leading to the arrest of Paul and Silas.

As was customary, the authorities had Paul and Silas stripped and beaten and then thrown into jail for the night. Rather than being intimidated, the evangelists spent the night singing hymns and praying. During the night, an earthquake shook the prison, and at once all the prison doors flew open, and all of the prisoners' chains came loose. The jailer, knowing he would be executed for any prisoners who escaped, was prepared to take his own life when Paul and Silas stopped him, assuring him that no prisoner had escaped. The man fell at their feet and asked how he could be saved. They replied, "Believe in the Lord Jesus and you will be saved—you and your household" (v. 31). The jailer received Christ, cleaned up their wounds and together they waited for the dawn (vv. 22–37).

When Paul and Silas were ordered released in the morning, they shared that they were Roman citizens. The beatings and humiliation they endured the night before were highly illegal, causing the magistrate tremendous anxiety. So the city leaders had the two given a proper escort out of town. Paul and Silas made a brief visit to Lydia's house and then continued their journey (vv. 35–40).

The fledgling church continued to grow while remaining closely connected to Paul. The great apostle had relationships with many churches, but the Philippians had won a special place in his heart. Writing from prison, he wanted to make sure that potentially the last words he could share on earth included his beloved Philippians, the namesake of his epistle to them.

When the letter was received, it would have been read aloud, as the literacy rate in the Roman Empire was less than 15 percent. Because of conditioning, people in the ancient world were accustomed to committing large amounts of verbally transmitted information to memory. This was not only because few could read, but because of the relative scarcity and expense of owning handwritten manuscripts. Reading Philippians out loud in one sitting will give one some idea of the effect it would have had with the first-century believers.

Life for Christians in Philippi would not have been easy, as indicated by the content of the letter. A growing antipathy toward the young Christian movement was spreading rapidly throughout the known world, fueled by the opposition of many of the Jewish faith and by factors as outlined below.

Features that were particularly challenging to the newly established church included:

1. *Emperor worship*—a part of the salutation to Caesar during toasts and expressions of homage was the honoring of him as "savior" and "lord." Since Christians would only honor Christ as Savior and Lord, believers were in conflict with accepted practice.

Caesars also claimed for themselves the status of being gods, complete with temples, priests, and ceremonies. As with the salutation to Caesar, citizens were expected to worship at these temples as part of their patriotic duty. Christians could not participate, which further added to the suspicion regarding their loyalties.

2. *Integration of pagan religions in everyday life*—it was not only emperor worship and veneration that were problematic. Also at conflict was the culture's expectation that at public meetings, as well as at club and trade union gatherings, the celebration feasts were held in dedication to particular gods, to which all in attendance were expected to pay homage. The Christians abstaining from these celebrations further formented hostility.

3. *Lack of significant Jewish presence*—only fifteen Jewish males were needed to form a synagogue in a locale, but Philippi had such a small Jewish population that no synagogue existed. Although this might have been considered an advantage because of widespread Jewish opposition to the gospel, the small number of Jews in Philippi worked against them as well. In cities that had a significant Jewish presence, the local population became aware of their belief in only one God and their allegiance to the Scriptures, as well as their refusal to participate in some civic events. In many places, the Jewish presence had paved the way for Christians to follow with at least some

basis of knowledge locally. This was not the case in Philippi. Everything about Christianity was new and strange to the populace.

Although the book of Philippians is a treasured letter in our New Testament, not much is heard of the church in Philippi after the death of Paul. Perhaps despite his pleading, the problems in the church were not resolved. It may be that some of the enemies Paul warned about gained a foothold and neutralized the church. Whether any of this happened, there was a time when the Philippian church was a shining example of witness in a difficult setting and its spirit captured the apostle Paul's heart.

PART 1

OF SLAVES
AND SERVICE

PHILIPPIANS 1:1–17

1

PHILIPPIANS 1:1-2

George MacDonald was quoted to say, "I would rather be what God chose to make me than the most glorious creature that I could think of. For to have been thought about—born in God's thought—and then made by God, is the dearest, grandest, and most precious thing in all thinking."[1] It was a similar thought that caused Paul to identify himself and Timothy as "servants of Christ Jesus."

Paul could have easily gone another direction. As he said later in the letter, he was a "Hebrew of the Hebrews," since he could trace his pure lineage back through the centuries. Or he could have spoken about his superior education at the feet of the esteemed teacher Gamaliel. He could have spoken about being a Roman citizen with all its privileges and protections. Instead, he chose to call himself a servant, more properly, a slave.

In the Roman Empire, slaves were of no account. Peter Chrysolgus wrote, "Whatever a master does to a slave, undeservedly, in anger, willingly, unwillingly, in forgetfulness, after careful thought, knowingly, unknowingly, is judgment, justice, and law."[2] Many of those who were slaves were captives of war, and so a slave might have originated from a higher social status than his or her master. Regardless of their background, in the Roman Empire social stratas, slaves occupied the lowest rung of the ladder. The significant difference for Paul was servanthood was the position he chose for himself, rather than having it imposed.

This submission represented his glad abandonment of status so he could serve, first Christ Jesus and then the people of God. In writing to his friends in Philippi, he constantly returned to this theme of abandonment to the lowest place of service in order to glorify God in the highest. Every blow he took, every hour in prison, every slander, every arduous exertion for the grateful as well as for those who betrayed him was an act of a self-appointed slave in service to Jesus Christ.

While taking this low position for himself, Paul called the Philippians by the highest status any believer could attain: "God's holy people." They were holy because they were set apart for the service of God. They were holy because they demonstrated the Spirit's infilling. They were holy because they evidenced the fruit of the Spirit. It did not matter what they had been, their racial or cultural background, whether they were slave or free. The grace of God had made them into something different.

While this status awakened them to their full potential, at the same time it put them at odds with the world. This was no weak-kneed, whispered profession of faith, but rather a full, determined opening of the heart for God to do His work whatever the consequences might be. While living a holy life put them in the line of fire, at the same time it provided the shield for their souls.

Perhaps you have heard of or even attended a funeral of some widely-recognized scoundrel, and yet he or she was extolled as the saintliest of people whose very breath caused flowers to grow in a barren land. To comfort the family, a new history is created not based on reality, but on how they wished the deceased had been. In this fiction, grace would not be needed because the person was supposedly so lovable, so meritorious, that God could hardly wait to get them into heaven to join Him in setting the world right or perhaps to help God provide notes to the nightingale's song.

The truth is that even the supposed saintliest person is in desperate need of grace, a grace that can only be given by a God whose infinite love bridges the gap between His holiness and our innate sinfulness. Those moments when we see ourselves at our worst, when we catch ourselves thinking broken thoughts about fallen acts, we only confirm that we need this unfathomable thing called grace.

The Nuremburg trial of Nazi war criminals following the Second World War proved that otherwise civilized and upstanding people could be guilty of horrendous acts. Had we lived in that time in that place, how many of us would have stood alongside them? The depravity of the human race is such that there is always the potential for monsters within us. Grace is what makes the difference, and it is this grace that Paul called upon for the Philippians. They remembered previous acts that now, in light of God's glorious work in them, made them blush to recall. But grace had come. Mercy had flowed. Their lives were not marked by sin's shame, but grace's glorious song.

Paul also wished them peace. The traditional greeting among Jews even in the present is *Shalom*, meaning peace. It spoke not only of an absence of conflict, but of a wholesomeness and well-being. But it changed as it passed into use among Christians. Boice explained, "For in Christian speech Paul's word *charis* was always associated with the grace of God. Peace . . . in Paul's mouth it must always have some reference to the fruits of justification, the result of the reconciliation of the Christian with God."[3] When grace comes, peace is walking alongside, both the proof and blessing of grace in action.

Paul spoke of the highs and lows, of being a slave and a holy person, of being the worst without grace and overwhelmingly blessed because of grace. It is this tension that makes the Christian life not something to be dreaded but an adventure to be lived.

REFLECTION QUESTIONS

1. Paul referred to himself as a slave. How do you think he would refer to himself in the twenty-first century?

2. Think of one of your worst moments. What does that say about the operation of God's grace in your life today?

2

PHILIPPIANS 1:3–8

John Fawcett had the opportunity of a lifetime when he was called to serve a larger and wealthier church in London. Having accepted the position, he and his wife were packing their wagons when one by one the people of his church at Wainsgate came to bid him farewell. Moved by the tears of his people, Fawcett shared with his wife that he felt they shouldn't go. She agreed. They unpacked their wagons, notified the London church that they wouldn't be coming and stayed for a total of fifty-four years. It was from this deep fellowship that Fawcett penned the words:

> Blest be the tie that binds
> Our hearts in Christian love;
> The fellowship of kindred minds
> Is like to that above.[1]

Paul's affection for the Philippians was no more evident than in verse three and further evidenced throughout the letter. Among the spiritual truths he wanted his friends to grasp was the depth of his love and appreciation for them. While there were many who appreciated Paul, these Philippians had reached his heart. Convinced that this might well be his last opportunity to say anything to them, he focused on what he sensed were their deepest spiritual needs while at the same time pouring out his gratitude for all they had meant to him. Other churches had wavered, but the Philippian church had not only remained true, they sought ways to let Paul know they supported him.

While many will speak of their affection or pledge their loyalty in the days of smooth sailing, we remember those who come alongside when we despair of seeing the dawn, when the waves are overwhelming us. These are the memories that warmed Paul's heart when long, lonely hours of isolation might have mocked him for all he believed and stood for.

The joy he spoke of in verse four is the delight that is not a passing emotion but a firm attitude. As parents always delight in their child doing well, Paul found joy in thinking of these dear people. This joy is part and parcel of the Christian life. As Dean Flemming aptly quips, "A joyless Christian makes no more sense than a waterless ocean."[2]

Paul rejoiced about their partnership in the gospel (v. 5), not only by sharing financially with him but in their active participation in working toward the same goals in Christ. Like him, they sought to live for Christ. Like him, they actively witnessed, willing to labor and lose as need be. Like him, they were fully convinced there could be no other way. They did not just cheer him on; they were comrades in arms.

The partnership is clearly seen in the stand the Philippians took with Paul in spite of his imprisonment. There was no "out of sight, out of mind" attitude, but rather a drawing closer to him as they forged ahead with the proclamation of the gospel. Why? Because they shared in God's grace (v. 7). That grace of God did not only represent their standing in Christ, but was the cement of their relationship with each other. They represented widely different backgrounds, but grace was the common ground, the blood that pulsated through their souls and his.

This brought Paul great joy tempered with a touch of sadness for not being with them as he sat in prison. He wrote, "I long for all of you with the affection of Christ Jesus" (v. 8). Our hope for eternal life promises the light of joy without the shadow of melancholy that often accompanies emotions in this life.

The primary relationship of the Christian is with Christ, but God provides the richness of additional fellowship with other believers. While we accept that no one knows us nor understands us as God does, at the same time we need the human touch, the reassuring voice, the connection we have with the heart of another sharing our pilgrimage. Paul shows that this deep affection is not the exception but the norm of our life in Christ.

REFLECTION QUESTIONS

1. How does the fellowship in Christ differ from your other friendships?

2. Can you think of a time when someone unexpectedly reached out to you in your time of need? Why do you think he or she did that?

PHILIPPIANS 1:6

On May 21, 1972, a man who later was confirmed to be insane jumped the barrier at St. Peter's Basilica in Vatican City and with a hammer attacked Michelangelo's "Pieta," the priceless statue of Mary holding the crucified Christ's limp body on her lap. The man struck the statue fifteen times, damaging Mary's elbow and wrist, shattering the fingers on one hand as well damaging her nose, veil, and left cheek. Under Dr. Deoclecio Redig de Campos, a team of seven scientists and restorers painstakingly gathered over two hundred chips that lay on the floor and, using microscopes, dental drills, and other tools, worked over four months to repair the statue. The results of their work, well hidden from the naked eye, allowed the Pieta to once again occupy its place of honor.

In a far more meticulous and divine manner, God has been at work in you since the hour you first believed. Paul shared, "He who began a good work in you will carry it on to completion until the day of Christ Jesus" (v. 6). The good work refers to the redemption and building up that God continued to do in the life of the believer beginning with the experience of salvation. There is a sense in which the work of salvation is complete the moment someone turns to Christ, so that even if it is a deathbed conversion, one can nevertheless be assured of eternal salvation. But there is also a very real sense in which salvation is a constantly expanding, continuous work of rebuilding what God does in someone through every day of his or her life.

If I blow up a balloon halfway, it is full of air. But as I put more air into it, though the balloon is larger we still say it is full of air. The capacity has changed, but the fullness is there all along. It is the same in the life of a Christian. God is continuing to build our capacity, our understanding—He is maturing us, molding us, conforming us to the image of Christ. Salvation occurs not only in a point in time but in the steady work of God done in us until He receives us unto Himself.

The glory of what God does in this good work is that He does not make us good as new but better than we ever could have otherwise been. Our fallen nature is such that, despite our best efforts, despite our most concentrated efforts at refinement and self-improvement, we will hit a ceiling. As with a rocket, to get beyond the surly bands of earth, we must have help beyond our own gravity of sin—something other than our own positive mental attitude.

In salvation God not only launches us but propels us to our destination. Along the way, if we allow Him, He uses each experience to mold and repair the damage sin has chipped away from our souls—to reform us into God's original design for us, taking us far beyond anything we could be ourselves. Every joy, every disappointment, every ache, and every success can be sanctified as the Holy Spirit works in the recesses of our hearts, teaching us, leading us, transforming us. The events of our lives are what God's Spirit uses as the building materials of our souls.

In the experience of holiness, we yield the building process to the Holy Spirit. Our experience of salvation redeems us, while our sanctification allows us to give away our limitations to God's fullness.

Rather than trying to get God to bless what we think is best, we want what He wants. Nothing more. Nothing less. Nothing else.

REFLECTION QUESTIONS

1. In what ways has God been doing His work in you?

2. The author says that God can use "every joy, every disappointment, every ache, and every success" to do His work in us. Can you recall something in your life that seemed outside the will of God yet proved that God was at work in you?

4

PHILIPPIANS 1:9–11

Cubic zirconia is a synthesized material that is optically flawless, colorless, and hard. In some ways superior to a real diamond, a cubic zirconia gem can be passed off as a natural diamond unless examined by an expert. By skilled inspection it will be revealed that cubic zirconia fails to be as hard or have the same weight as natural diamonds. Beautiful as they are, they are not the real thing. Paul, writing to his Philippian friends, wanted their lives to stand up to examination as genuine.

Having told the Philippians that he thanked God every time he remembered them, Paul shared the content of his prayers on their behalf. He spoke first of love, using the word for a deep kindred fellowship that overflows with goodwill and kindness, continually growing, ready to meet every circumstance—even misunderstanding.

The Bible always sees righteousness as being about love, and this love is something more than emotion. It also fully engages the intellect and the will. Over all things it is an intelligent, insightful love. True love is not some sentimental infatuation that yanks a person up one minute and down the next. Instead it chooses to love a person regardless of strengths or weaknesses. It seeks to see another's best potential realized, even if that means taking a back seat to make it happen (see 1 Cor. 13).

This kind of love gives discernment. The Greek term Paul used came from the testing of money to ensure it was genuine, not counterfeit. Few things are more devastating than love falsely proclaimed in order to manipulate another. Paul said that the kind of love he was speaking of allowed for discernment to gauge what was best in the life of the believer.

Purity was added to the list. The original word was also translated *sincere*. Dr. James Boice explained:

> Dishonest dealers were in the habit of filling in the cracks with a hard pearly wax that would blend in with the color of the pottery. This made the cracks practically undetectable . . . when the pottery was held up to the light, especially the sun. It was said that the artificial element was detected by "sun-testing." Honest dealers marked their finer products by the caption *sine cera*—"without wax."[1]

So it is that a holy person is what he or she appears to be: one whose life can stand up to inspection. This is a life that is pure and blameless, which, as we saw in the previous verses, can only be accomplished by the "good work" of God's Holy Spirit carrying on in our lives (v. 6).

Of course, blameless is not the same as faultless. We live in fallen bodies, with minds that have been scarred by original (independence from God) and voluntary sin. Although we are cleansed, the consequential scars of sin require the ongoing repair process by God's Spirit within us. Though flawed in our own flesh, we can be blameless in Christ.

For instance, a believer can fully love and serve God to the best of his or her ability, and yet find that inherent limitations still result in mistakes and misunderstanding. A man may testify with no thought other than to glorify God, but in the process say something that hurts or offends another. He may well be blameless but not faultless. The true intent will be revealed for all our actions in the "day of Christ" though never fully understood in this world, but we praise God because He knows our hearts and our intent, and that will shine through even the faultiest ways we seek to serve Him or express ourselves.

The result is that we are "filled with the fruit of right-eousness." That righteousness does not originate in us but is implanted in us through the Holy Spirit's work in our hearts. It allows us to take on the role of the slave in order to serve others, to take up our cross and follow Christ. It takes for its example the righteousness of Christ, refusing to be distracted by those who might fall at our side or those in prominence who might fail.

This is for the glory and praise of God. The very best thing that can be said of any follower of Christ is how he or she lives glorifies God.

Reading about this should make us pause to ask God if we would bear up to close examination. And when we see how we may fall short, we must acknowledge that the failing is not merely in our performance, but in our failure to rely upon the workings of God's Holy Spirit in us. Pause now, ask the Holy Spirit to search your heart and reveal to you any falseness, any unworthiness, any attitude or practice that stands in the way of you being all that God intends.

REFLECTION QUESTIONS

1. In what ways can love engage our thought, emotion, and will?

2. How can a person be at fault but blameless at the same time?

5

PHILIPPIANS 1:12–17

Paul's imprisonment was more than an inconvenience. By appealing to Caesar (see Acts 25:1–12), Paul was destined to meet one of the most notorious villains of the ancient world. Nero started off well enough as supreme ruler of the Roman Empire, but he found power intoxicating. As he progressed in his reign, he became increasingly more corrupt and cruel, finally becoming a living embodiment of evil. Although never proven, it is generally accepted that in order to build a more glorious Rome, he committed arson to clear out areas where he wanted to make improvement. When the fire blazed out of control, he blamed the despised and misunderstood Christians. Part of his punishment of them included dipping some in pitch and setting them on fire to light his garden at night. It was in this man's hands that Paul sought justice.

Paul was realistic about the uncertainty of his fate. But even with the possibility of his death in view, he saw God at work through all circumstances. In verse 12, he said that what had happened had advanced the gospel. The original Greek for the word *advance* was a military term referring to the team of soldiers who set about clearing trails and building roads so the army could follow. Paul noted that this advance was not in spite of what had happened to this point but rather that the circumstances were the wherewithal by which God made things happen. These were not stumbling blocks in the path, but building blocks to accomplish God's will for him and others.

The injustice of his imprisonment was obvious, even to the guards (v. 13). They knew why he was there. Paul had not committed acts of violence or led an insurrection. He was there only because he chose to live for Christ. Even with false charges that stole his freedom, there remained the clarity of his witness about the power of Christ to transform. While we do not know if any guards were converted under his prison ministry, they did hear the message of the gospel. It was customary for a guard to be chained to a prisoner all the time. The rotations of guards for this duty would mean that different guards sat with Paul for hours at a time. We cannot imagine that this great evangelist let the prime opportunity of witnessing to the guards pass. Paul was not out of place, but felt he was appointed to be here. What appeared to be a hopeless situation was instead a mission field.

A beautiful by-product occurred when those outside the prison walls took advantage of their freedom to proclaim Christ. And as Dr. Richard R. Melick, Jr. noted, "The context assumes their preaching was encouraged by the imprisonment, not by the expected release."[1] The suffering provided inspiration, not Paul's possible deliverance! And the hallmark of what made their good works authentic was . . . love (v. 16).

Some of the struggle with sincerity within the early church is seen in verses 15–17. Paul had enemies, not just among the Jewish leaders, but among fellow believers as well. Paul noted that some preached Christ with counterfeit motives—envy, rivalry, and selfish ambition. How could God use those with selfish ambition? Dr. Ben Witherington, III notes, "The proclamation of the true Word does not require a perfect messenger; God can write straight with crooked lines."[2] Somehow, even through unworthy motives, the power of the gospel, fueled by the Holy Spirit, accomplished that which glorified God.

Others were more benevolent. They saw in Paul an ally who now was paying the price for refusing to renounce his Lord. They likely deemed that, while Paul was taking care of the inside, they were taking care of the outside. If Paul could stay faithful in the bleakest of circumstances, if he could be true there, then they had no excuse to shy away from their own witness. The faithful follower does not wait for a big moment or large stage to act. He or she looks at the moment and uses the raw materials at hand.

This challenges us to think of how we act with the opportunities God has given to us. God does not want for us to relegate our committed service to the unknown "someday" or for us to witness when there is the right convergence of circumstances. Following Paul's example, He wants us to take advantage of what He has placed at our disposal. If we have bricks, we use bricks. If we have sticks, we use sticks, always keeping in mind that none of it is any good without the Holy Spirit's blessing. Nothing is unworthy if He sanctifies it.

REFLECTION QUESTIONS

1. Is it better to wait on God before witnessing or to go ahead and speak out in the moment?

2. Paul said that, regardless of people's motives, Christ was preached; and he was happy about it. What might make a difference when the falseness of the one preaching Christ undermines the gospel?

PART 2

LOFTY
LOWLINESS

PHILIPPIANS 2:1–11

6

PHILIPPIANS 2:1–2

The ancient Greek storyteller Aesop told the story of a lion that watched carefully each day for an opportunity to feast on three bulls that shared a pasture. The bulls were the strongest of friends, each coming to the other's aid, thus leaving the lion no hope of ever attacking them successfully. Realizing this, the lion approached each bull secretly, telling him that the others had slandered him or considered themselves better than him. It wasn't long until the bulls argued, went to different pastures so they wouldn't see each other, and with that, became easy prey for the lion.

The love Paul had for the church in Philippi sings through the entire letter. The words *joy* and *rejoicing* are mentioned fifteen times, more than in any other book of the Bible. But it was not a perfect church. With all that was going right, there was still an underlying current of disunity.

And Paul knew that this infection could spread and be fatal.

It would seem that if people share a common salvation they would naturally be unified. However, salvation does not destroy our temperament or wipe away our knowledge or experiences, nor does it program us to sense, act, believe, or think identically to our fellow believers. Unity does not mean uniformity.

Often the ironic reality will be that, for the very reason that we care deeply about the work of God, we will differ on how it is best accomplished. And, after all, the person who gives thoughtless agreement likely does not comprehend what is being talked about or simply doesn't care. Unity is not to be gained at the expense of truth, and less so at the expense of love. There can be agreement in a mob, for instance, but that does not mean it is doing the truly loving thing.

The difference between unity and uniformity is key. Imagine a symphony orchestra that gathered with all the instruments playing only the same note. What could be more boring? Instead, each instrument plays its own part while the others play theirs. The differences create richer, deeper chords and harmonies. The instrumentalists, while paying attention to their own music, are also keenly aware of the conductor and the other instruments. At one time they might be silent while another section takes prominence. At another, it might be their time to carry the melody or shine with a solo part. Through it all an orchestra shares the same priority as each part moves together to the finish—it is unified, not uniform. In the same way, God wants each believer to employ his or her gifts as each has ability and opportunity, moving together toward a common goal.

Where Christian unity is authentically displayed is in a common love of the Lord and, consequently, love and appreciation for other believers. This is not to mean some people won't rub us wrong. For one reason or another, there are some personalities or something about someone's approach that bothers us. But for the sake of Christ and the unity of His body, we choose to love and appreciate what that person brings to the table. In doing so, we can realize that there are likely those who are making the same allowances for us.

In addition, there is appreciation for different gifts and abilities employed for the same great overall goal. Paul dealt with this issue with the Corinthians when he reminded them that we are all like different parts of the body, performing different functions but all making valuable contributions to the whole (see 1 Cor. 12:12–30).

What do we do when disunity exists? Paul urged the Philippians to move away from scrutinizing what is wrong with the other guy and toward lifting our eyes toward Christ. Those differences and annoyances melt as we focus and rely upon Christ, fan into flame our love for Him, and remember that the reason we exist as a body at all is because of His redemption and keen interest in who and whose we are.

REFLECTION QUESTIONS

1. Think of a time when disunity occurred where you were. How was it resolved? Was this the biblical standard?

2. How are you playing your part in God's orchestra?

7

PHILIPPIANS 2:3–5

It has been reported that the great holiness preacher, Commissioner Samuel Logan Brengle, almost left The Salvation Army early on. Sent to London to train to be an officer, he was at that time the most highly educated man in the fledgling movement. Expecting that his superior education would come with some privileges, he was shocked to find himself sitting in front of a stack of men's boots he was to polish while others were involved in street ministry. He nearly walked away, but then he heard the Lord whisper to him, "If I was willing to wash the dirty feet of the disciples, should you not be willing to polish a few boots?" Ashamed at his pride but inspired by the insight, he found great joy as he worked his way through the pile of muddy, smelly boots.

Philippians 2:3 contrasts two sets of attitudes. Paul speaks of the negatives: selfishness and conceit. The Greek idea behind selfishness is that of a person who insists on having his or her own way. It is the person who pushes to the head of the line, who jockeys to be noticed. *Conceit*, as Karl Barth interprets the original language, means "decking oneself out with an appearance that has nothing behind it."[1] We know conceit when we see it in others because of how we are pushed down or disregarded. What is not as apparent is when it is operating in us.

Paul's call to humility was as counter-cultural in his day as in ours. With our tongues we'll laud humility, but what still lingers in our minds is that odious word *meek*. It feels like the servility expected of a slave, inferiority not only in attitude but in fact. Our instincts tell us that humility means to count for nothing at all. Among non-Christians in the Roman Empire, there was hardly an attitude that would be less desirable to emulate.

The coming of Christ redeemed the idea of humility by His own example of servanthood. The stark difference between His glorious resurrection and the scene a few days before when He knelt before the dirty feet of the disciples to wash them was difficult to reconcile. But this example was to be lived out among believers as part of the demonstration of the total change that comes in the life of a Christian. Any believer who seriously desires to have a heart's "attitude the same as Christ Jesus" must begin where God the Son's heart has always been: humility.

Clearly this godly ideal of humility is not one of groveling or self-loathing, no more than it could have been God the Son's attitude. We don't despise the gifts that God has given us or fail to use them. Rather, we are so assured in who we are before God that we can easily look out for the interests of others before our own. If I am standing at the plate, I should not be ashamed to swing the bat with all my might and feel joy if I hit a homerun. But neither should I demean the skill of the other team's player who dashes my dreams with a brilliant catch.

Humility is proven by our readiness to prioritize other people's interests rather than clinging to our fleshly survival instincts of protecting our own. The same love that allows a mother to clean up messy diapers, when a few years earlier she would have turned aside in disgust at the sight of them, should be evident in we who are in Christ as we deal with other people without a thought about what we deserve (because it is irrelevant). Our profession is more proven in the messiness and inconvenience that come in the moment-by-moment humdrum of life, far more than in our public successes. Humility accepts both the mundane and the special opportunities equally as times to show forth a witness to the transformed life we have in Christ (that is, promoting the interests of others. It's God's will we want to be done, not our own).

In Alcoholics Anonymous, there is frequent reference to "stinking thinking." It refers to destructive thought patterns or telling oneself lies, resulting in alcoholics returning to their abuse of alcohol. An essential part of recovery is not only abstinence from a substance but a fundamental internal change in thought processes. Abstinence alone, without changed thinking, is not only likely to be unsuccessful but can allow a person to substitute one addictive substance for another.

Paul addressed this same issue with the Christians in Philippi. If they were to understand what it was to live a holy life that pleased God, it would involve more than an outward change of behavior. The standard was high: "Have the same mind-set as Christ Jesus" (v. 5).

The believer is to have the attitude, outlook, and character of Christ—that is, humility. *The New American Commentary* notes that the original Greek would best be rendered, "Think this in you which Christ thought in him."[2] There is a loftiness and grandeur in this humility that fairly takes the breath away. We are to think humbly of others' interests above our own, just like Christ did and does! It hearkens to one of Paul's most famous statements in Romans: "Do not conform to the pattern of this world, but be transformed by the renewing of your mind. Then you will be able to test and approve what God's will is—his good, pleasing and perfect will" (12:2). Conformity to the world's way of thinking is self-promotion; transformed thinking into Christ's character promotes others.

What exactly does having this humble mind of Christ look like? Paul spent the next few verses explaining what that was.

REFLECTION QUESTIONS

1. Who has been an example of humility to you? Why?

2. Take a moment to list the things you can do well as well as the things you cannot. Focus on both lists. How do you feel after thinking about these things?

8

PHILIPPIANS 2:6–7

After telling the Philippians they were to have the mind of Christ, Paul then shared one of the greatest Christological passages in Scripture. Some feel it was a hymn of the early church because of its poetic quality. Regardless of its origin or function, no pinnacle of praise exceeds it in theological depth or poetic grandeur.

Paul spoke of Jesus, "Who, being in very nature God, did not consider equality with God something to be used to his own advantage" (2:6). It was important to establish that Christ did not aspire nor did He somehow elevate Himself to a higher position. His nature was authentically that of God and as such, He was the truest and fullest expression of God, in human form. What He had already was not something to be grasped—He didn't need to cling to His status because of who He was and is.

Satan, in contrast, grasped after what he was not, and with no interest in unity. We remember that Satan's fall was because he sought to be equal to God, with no interest in being with God. But Jesus, as part of the three-in-one that is the holy Godhead from all eternity, was so equal with God as to be one with the other persons of the Trinity; that is, triune—three distinct persons, yet so profoundly united as to literally be the one person of God. That kind of unity in God's self-contained, loving community was the basis for Jesus's mind-set—the model of humility for His church.

The setting aside of the advantages of His divine form constituted a sacrifice that allowed in His incarnation not only Christ's taking on human flesh and form, but taking upon Himself a reduction that humans themselves could not fathom. The Creator became His created. The Author became one of His story's characters.

What we celebrate at Christmas was the beginning of the emptying of Himself. The omnipotent, omniscient, omnipresent God became a finite, a time and place con-strained body with tiny, fragile limbs that could not control themselves and with absolute dependence upon the help of others. He whose breath formed humanity, sentenced Himself to a body with all the same human foibles, bruises, sniffles, and frustrations we all have while we are in this mortal flesh.

Paul was clear that this humility practiced by God was self-imposed—He "made Himself nothing." And what's more, He did this because of who He was. "Being in very nature God," the Creator's reducing Himself to "nothing" for the sake of His creatures must be part and parcel to His very nature. If we could imagine shrinking to become an amoeba, we might have an inkling of what Jesus faced when our all-knowing Creator made Himself a child who would have to grow, not only in physical stature, but remarkably "in wisdom," and even more remarkably, "in favor with God," as well as in favor with His now-fellow humans (Luke 2:52).

Even here, Jesus might have at least given Himself a favored position within some royal family where (one might think) His miracles and teachings would have a more ready audience to see Him for who He was. Surely Rome, not Nazareth; Athens, not Bethlehem would have been the preferred stages to present Himself. But no. He sought the lowest place, taking on the form of a slave. As indicated earlier, slaves occupied the bottom rung in the world. And He chose to be there, below every other place.

If we hope to have the mind-set of Christ, we must dwell on what this humility that is in God's very nature truly is—what it means for us. An athlete might in a way empty him- or herself to win a race. But Christ emptied Himself to lose our life's race by being killed—a tragically humiliating death. He set aside His glory and privilege to be used and abused. Rather than seeking blessings, He came for beatings.

Rather than seeking out relationships for support, He chose people He knew would fail and betray Him. Rather than seeking comfort, He chose the splinters of a manger, a carpenter's shop, and a cross.

REFLECTION QUESTIONS

1. Imagine God the Son before reducing Himself to the point of being conceived by Mary. What thoughts come to mind when you consider He knew He would have to grow in wisdom, from human infancy?

2. Can you think of any human analogy where someone abandoned an advantaged position to seek a lower place? How does this compare with Christ? How is it like Jesus? How is it different?

9

PHILIPPIANS 2:8

As Paul continued to explore what humble servanthood meant for Christ, he described it in terms of His obedience to death.

You and I have no choice regarding death. Should the Lord tarry, we will all take our final breath and, with but few exceptions, will not have the choice of when or where that might be. That is a sobering thought we all must learn to face. But in the case of Jesus, there was a choice. The previous verses outlined the divinity of Christ that included His eternal nature. As One who was truly God and thus eternal, the termination of life was totally foreign to the divine nature.

He would even taste our death, the consequence of our sin, though He was sinless. Our deaths would have satisfied God's law and justice, but then God (the Son) took upon

Himself sin's consequence of death. In His coming to earth with all the sacrifice that entailed, there was yet more. Though sinless, He died the death of sinners. While the limitation of the human body was alien to the nature of God, how much more this must have been to the Author of life! His loving obedience was absolute, proven by making the choice to die. Humanity, being sinful and separated from God, had no choice but to die. Disobedience in this regard was not an option. But God the Son's humility was such that, though He could choose to justly impose it, He instead chose to obey it in our place.

Greater than this was not only that He chose to die, but He chose how and when that was to happen. *How* was what stunned both the Jews and the Gentiles. No crueler and more painful death was known to humankind than crucifixion. Although crucifixion had existed for hundreds of years, the cold calculation of the Romans had perfected it so that it exacted supreme agony while prolonging it to the limits of what the body could endure, inflicting the victim with the most extreme humiliation. So fearsome was crucifixion that Roman citizens could not, by law, be crucified, regardless of the crime they committed. It was reserved for outsiders, for career criminals, for the traitor and the slave. This is why Paul emphasized the degree of Christ's obedience: "obedient unto death—even death on a cross."

The horror of the cross was not lost on the early Christians.

The early symbol of their faith was primarily a fish, not a cross. Indeed, that first generation of Christians would have been shocked that so cruel a means of execution would in any way find a place of honor. They would be even more surprised at what we have done to the cross by miniaturizing it, casting it in gold, encrusting it with jewels, and smoothing all the splinters away. For a cross to be worn as jewelry would be as shocking to them as it would be for us to encounter someone in our day wearing a guillotine necklace, executioner axe earrings, or encountering a hangman's noose on a worship table. A cross was the worst form of punishment that could be mustered. Although there is certainly nothing wrong with wearing crosses as jewelry, especially if it is meant to be a witness, we would do well to ponder the offensive nature of this form of execution to all who lived in the days of Jesus.

Paul's point in all of this was that, because the plight of humanity was clearly hopeless, the solution must be one so grand, so expansive that nothing less would be enough. And so Jesus came, not as the new caesar, but as a tiny boy, not in Rome or Athens, but in Bethlehem; not schooled at the feet of the most brilliant philosophers, but by meditating in a carpenter's shop after attending a little synagogue in the backwater town of Nazareth.

His fame would not come on the field of battle with troops shouting His name as He charged against the enemy, but by leprous hands that stretched out for healing and blind eyes that sought to view Him in their first sight. It was down, down, down to the depths of a slave and a slave's service. And when death came, it would be preceded by betrayal, accentuated by the abandonment of His friends, punctuated by a thorny crown pushed upon His brow. He would be led to the most public place, not to be mourned as much as mocked. And the cross. No person had been more unjustly or cruelly betrayed by the ones He came to save nor suffer more exquisitely as His body was wracked in agony and the Father turned His back on Him. The Author and Creator of all life, "obedient to death—even death on a cross."

REFLECTION QUESTIONS

1. What would be your reaction if you met someone wearing a guillotine on a necklace? Is that reaction similar or different from how people in the first century reacted to the cross?

2. Is there any way that God could prove Himself more humble than He did?

10

PHILIPPIANS 2:9–11

In order to unite the empire as well as emphasize their power and glory, the caesars increasingly allowed and then encouraged that they be worshiped. While seeking a glory that was not theirs, the foolishness of their deification was evident when one died or was deposed. The temples erected in their honor were quickly converted to accommodate the new emperor, their statues were taken down and destroyed, and in some cases, efforts were made to expunge their names from official records. In the sharpest of contrasts, the growing movement of Christians worshiped Jesus Christ, whose glory was not coveted, but sacrificed, His power curbed instead of abused, His divine nature not a means of propaganda, but a revealing of the full Trinity.

After outlining Christ's abdication of His divine advantages for a time, Paul reminded believers that the splendor of the

Savior was revealed. First, there was His exaltation. "God highly exalted Him to the highest place and gave him the name that is above every name" (v. 9). The place He was lifted to was actually an acknowledgement of His return, to assume all that He had denied Himself while accepting the limits of human existence. He could only be restored to His former glory because as the unlimited God, no greater glory existed.

In these verses there are two references to His name. First, the "name that is above every name" (v. 9), and then we were told that all would submit to "the name of Jesus" (v. 10). In our modern thinking it is easy to skip by these references to the name of Jesus. But in ancient times, names were tremendously significant. Names stated the hopes of parents as they named their child. Whenever there were significant events in a place, a name was given to commemorate what happened. Several Bible characters received their names as a result of divine revelation, including Jesus. The name of God was considered so holy it was seldom used, and in our Bibles, God's proper name, *YHWH*, was almost never used, translators choosing instead to use the term, *Lord*. What was communicated by Paul was the name of Jesus was of the greatest significance, so much so that at the end of the age, it is to His name that all of creation will bow in absolute submission.

The power and glory of the Savior is acknowledged by the reaction to His full revealing in the last day. To Him "every knee should bow, in heaven and on earth and under the earth, and every tongue acknowledge that Jesus Christ is Lord, to the glory of God the Father" (vv. 10–11). It is staggering just thinking of the moment when humanity lays aside everything else to kneel before Him in worship. Unity that has been so elusive in the world will be an accomplished fact as every person will at once recognize Christ as Lord. Those living at the time will be joined in adoration and worship by all who have ever lived. That number will be comprised of all living creatures, including Satan and the fallen angels. Should life exist in other places in the universe, even those beings will join the throng. The caesars and the kings, dictators, and presidents will kneel next to beggars and outsiders. All will be involved in their highest possible pursuit—submission to and worship of Jesus Christ as Lord.

This act of worship will not be the sad submission of a vanquished foe, but a moment of high praise, thanksgiving and joy beyond any known in the present life. We were created to glorify God. In that moment, we will realize we are at our best when we offer our best to Him.

REFLECTION QUESTIONS

1. If all will eventually recognize Jesus as Lord anyway, what benefit is it to honor Him now in this life?

2. What does the name of Jesus mean to you?

PART 3

SHINING
BRIGHTLY

PHILIPPIANS 2:12–30

PHILIPPIANS 2:12–13

The widow of Zarephath who aided Elijah was, at the time of his arrival, making preparations for the last meal for her and her son (see 1 Kings 17:7–16). Elijah interrupted with a seemingly impossible and calloused demand. She was to feed him and give him something to drink with the promise that, if she did so, God would provide for her. She obeyed, and God did indeed supply what she needed until the crisis was over.

Couldn't God have provided for her without this test of faith? Certainly. But this is one more instance of God partnering with people to accomplish His will and blessing. The Bible is strewn with these partnerships that cause us to marvel at God's way among His people.

In these verses Paul instructed the Philippians to "work out your salvation with fear and trembling" (v. 12). What did he mean by that? Isn't salvation the work of God?

Recalling that disunity was a problem among the Philippians, the apostle reminded them that their faith was not some private, secret thing of the heart, but it was meant to be lived out in all relationships and situations. Work out means to live out our salvation. The current climate in the Western world dictates that the things of faith should be kept in their own segregated sphere, preferably to an allotted hour on Sunday morning. The prevailing view is that the business, political, and social world should be untainted by the influence of Christian love. This flies in the face of the biblical teaching that our faith is not only something that is to permeate every area of our lives, but if it fails to do so, it is useless. In his epistle, James launched a frontal assault on that kind of thinking (see James 2:14–26).

This is especially true in the church. We are given no pass to love only the people who are not prickly or to segregate ourselves, gathering in holy huddles among those who share our values and beliefs. Living with people is by its nature difficult. Even the most gregarious person finds that others sometimes bother him or her. And because we all possess a variety of personalities, there will always be people whose differences seem to give them direct access to our spinal cord to attack that last calm nerve. However, if we of the church fail in living out our salvation among fellow believers, we have no right to claim our gospel can change the world.

Beyond that application, working out our salvation also means that, in addition to the initial experience of conversion, we find that God's Holy Spirit continues to show us where change is needed, where He might lead us to greater insight, and how we might employ ourselves for His glory. The new believer and the most aged saint share this in common: they are working out their salvation in their everyday.

That God is at work is what makes working out salvation a possibility. This is not a "turn over a new leaf" kind of Christianity, but one of transformational renewal. Why? "It is God who works in you to will and to act in order to fulfill his good purpose" (v. 13).

No matter how accomplished, educated, experienced, or equipped we might be, we are all victims of the fall. We are born in sin, then choose to sin. Beyond the grief caused God by our disobedience, there is residual damage. If we injure ourselves, there is the immediate first aid that is applied, but in the healing process, a scar often remains as a reminder of what happened. In the same way, sin is not only an immediate transgression we commit, but something that often has long-term consequences.

As God works in us to do His good pleasure, He is reshaping us, banging out the dents, polishing away some of the scuffs . . . healing the scars. He is at work not only for our benefit in the moment, but to fit us for our eternal existence as citizens of the kingdom. Just as an infant forms in the mother's womb for a life outside, we are being fitted for a life that is far different than the one we live now.

If sin had never entered the world, we would be very different than we are now. God knows what our truest potential is, what we could have been had sin not been part of the equation. The Holy Spirit deals with sin and its consequences, whispering here and urging there, to put us back on the path of what we might have been, until one day, when we are glorified in His presence, we see what He has seen our possibility to be. We will stand in wonder at what He has done. It was not His good pleasure to abandon us at our worst, but to work with us and in us. "Dear friends, now we are children of God, and what we will be has not yet been made known. But we know that when Christ appears, we shall be like him, for we shall see him as he is" (1 John 3:2).

REFLECTION QUESTIONS

1. How are you working out your salvation?

2. How is God working in you according to His good purpose?

12

PHILIPPIANS 2:14–16

While on vacation a few years ago, we stopped to worship in a church we selected at random. It was a beautiful service with the pastor delivering a well-thought-out and practical message. As we were leaving we were greeted by one of the church members who immediately began to share what was wrong with the church, compared the present pastor with the previous one, and in so doing doused any sense of blessing we felt. Sadly, my experience is hardly unusual.

As Paul continued to deal with the Philippians regarding their problems within the church, he gave them a breathtaking command: "Do everything without grumbling or arguing" (v. 14). The all-inclusiveness of this command challenges even the saintliest. Clearly, however, Paul only stressed what he had already established as Christ's model of humility for the Christian, a mind-set that was to fill every moment and be evident in every situation that an individual faced.

Complaining refers to voiced discontentment. Arguing refers to more of a simmering, internal brooding and whispering to one another. This verse hearkened back to the grumbling or arguing done by the Israelites as they traveled through the wilderness to the Promised Land. Here they had daily evidence of God's provision through the manna in addition to numerous grand miracles that included water where there was none and meat that literally flew into their hands. The presence of the cloud by day and the pillar of fire by night were further proofs of God among them. Yet the children of Israel seemed to spend more time looking down than looking up. Although their complaining often garnered severe punishment, this seemed to be little deterrent. Paul was warning the Philippians not to be the modern equivalent of the Israelites in the wilderness.

Contrasting with these negatives was the admonition to be blameless and pure. These are hallmarks of the life of holiness.

As previously discussed, those living a holy life are to be blameless, but that is not the same as being faultless. We have limited minds and bodies, possess different personalities, were raised in different families, and live in various cultures. Despite our best efforts, we will not do everything perfectly or be faultless. While that may be true, our hearts can be blameless. I may give my testimony with horrible grammar and using crude expressions, but the love that motivates that testimony makes my heart blameless. The delivery is faulty, but the intention is blameless.

The Greek word for *pure* was also used to describe metal with no alloy. In the spiritual life, it speaks of a love that is not manipulative or diluted with self-interest. It gives without seeking payback or reward; it serves without thought of keeping a tally of favors in return. Again, the outside manner may not be perfect, but the heart cleansed by the Holy Spirit can be pure. The Bible clearly presented this, not as something only to be gained at death, but to be lived and enjoyed in the present life.

If we avoid grumbling and arguing and instead are blameless and pure, the inevitable result is that we will "shine like stars in the sky as you hold firmly to the word of life" (vv. 15–16). The state of the heart and the behaviors Paul described here produce the certain result of love shining against the backdrop of a dark world that by itself can at best produce only a murky dusk for light.

It is interesting that Paul did not command the believers to shine. It is inescapable if we are truly living out our love in Christ. The idea of hiding our light under a bushel is foreign to the one who is animated by the Holy Spirit. Our failure to shine is a denial of the Lord and a colossal abandonment of what we are to be in Christ. As Flemming remarked, "We have no possibility of changing the culture if we are too much like it."[1]

REFLECTION QUESTIONS

1. How do you measure up with Paul's command to "do everything without grumbling or arguing"?

2. In our present culture, how is it easier or more difficult to "shine like stars?"

13

PHILIPPIANS 2:17–18

The reference Paul made to being "poured out" was very familiar to the people of Philippi. Although also used in the Jewish religious practice of burnt offerings, that ritual would not have been as well known to Philippian Gentiles. So it is more likely Paul was referring to the Roman practice rather than the Jewish form of the ritual. Either way, it presented a very clear picture of Paul's understanding of how his life might end.

As part of the sacrificial system, the libation to be "poured out" as an offering was most commonly wine. There were three ways it was offered that may have been in Paul's thinking as he was writing. The first involved pouring the wine out on an empty altar by itself. In this application, it could mean Paul had offered to the Lord all that he was with nothing remaining.

The second involved the worshiper offering a costly sacrificial animal that would then be burned on the altar. As Dr. Boice described it, "Following this sacrifice, the ancient worshiper would make an additional offering called a libation. He would take a cup of wine and pour it on the altar, thus pouring it upon the sacrifice that was already burning. Because the altar was hot, the libation would immediately disappear in a puff of steam." Here the meaning would be that Paul was poured out like a libation on the crucified Christ, the sacrificial Lamb of God. Gladly adding his own life as a sacrifice, he rejoiced to see his life joined with his Lord's as he gave all he could offer.

The third was the use of the libation as a part of funeral rites. Here it showed a person's earthly life was spent, and as the body would return to the elements, so the wine was absorbed by the ground. Although this may have occurred to the first-century believers, its note of hopelessness did not at all represent the joyful Christian message.

Having spoken about the sacrificial nature of his impending death, Paul followed immediately with a declaration of his joy: "I am glad and rejoice with all of you. So you too should be glad and rejoice with me" (vv. 17–18).

This idea of being poured out was not the mutterings of a dejected, deserted, and defeated man, but rather it fueled his joy. Having served and suffered for the Savior he adored, to think that his life would culminate in offering, the absolute last that he had to give, was to Paul a wonderful comfort. While no one should desire or seek to be martyred, his joining in long line of martyrs through the ages who had met their deaths for the Savior was nevertheless cause for joy. Such a joy can only come out of the grace of God fully operative in a heart totally yielded to Him. The survival instinct is overcome by the knowledge that there is a joy higher, more sublime than clinging to a few more years of life in denial of it.

Few of us will be called upon to die in this manner. That some of the Philippians may have themselves died for their faith, there can be little doubt. But it is likely that most lived their lives until natural causes carried them to eternity. For those not called upon to pour themselves out in this manner, the pouring out of martyrs' lives—though tragic and sad—is ultimately encouraging in their own faith.

One of the profound impacts made by those first generations of Christians and many since then was the discovery that joy was not dependent upon circumstances. Our joy is not in getting what we want or accomplishing our goals, nor is it to be found in ticking off the things we wanted to do in life. Our joy is rooted in the Lord. As such, we have confidence that, since He is with us in everything, there is nothing that can exist where He cannot reach us and turn to blessing. Here, the one on her deathbed reflects a joyful radiance; there, though surrounded by enemies and poverty, the songs of praise are sung with enthusiasm. Our joy is never contingent upon what happens or what we possess — it springs unquenchably from the Lord.

REFLECTION QUESTIONS

1. How might your life be poured out before the Lord?
2. Have you ever had an occasion of joy when circumstances did not seem to warrant it? Why?

14

PHILIPPIANS 2:19–24

During the First World War, two young men named Mike and Joe, best friends from their youngest days, enlisted together in what they agreed was their patriotic duty. They were sent to the front where bloody and seemingly endless conflict caused troops from both sides to hurl themselves at each other, to die together on the no man's land that separated the lines.

During one of these charges and the subsequent retreat back to the trenches, Mike looked around for Joe. He heard Joe calling his name. Quickly, Mike jumped up to bring Joe back.

The sergeant yelled, "Don't go out there. He's a goner. There's nothing you can do."

Mike looked back, then charged forward to reach Joe amid bullets fired from the other side. A few minutes later,

Mike returned with Joe in his arms, but it was obvious that the reward for his bravery was a mortal wound. The sergeant rushed over and checked Joe's pulse, confirming he was already dead. Furious, he ran over to Mike and yelled, "I told you not to go. Joe is dead and now you're going to die. And for what?"

Mike lifted his head and said, "It was worth it. When I got to him, Joe said, 'I knew you'd come for me.'"

Just as God made us for fellowship with Him, He also made us for relationship with each other. For good reason, we need the touch of a human hand, the sound of a human voice; Paul was no different. This spiritual giant, whose truths have shaped our understanding of the Christian faith, needed a friend like Timothy. Although Paul was clearly the more prominent of the two as he served in a fatherly role, he found strength and encouragement in what Timothy had to offer. We can see some of this in how he commended his young friend to the Philippians.

"I have no one else like him, who will show a genuine concern for your welfare . . . you know that Timothy has proved himself, because as a son with his father he has served with me in the work of the gospel" (vv. 20–22).

The phrase that speaks the deepest of their friendship says, "I have no one else like him." In the ancient world, the idea of such close friendship was found in the Greek word Paul used, *isopsychos,* which means, "having one soul." The modern equivalent is to call someone a soulmate (even if it has become unfortunately clichéd). Perhaps the most common setting for this deep abiding friendship is within the context of a marriage in which the husband and wife are also best friends. Without compromising the sacred bonds of marriage, there can still be similarly close friendships outside of marriage such as that which Paul and Timothy enjoyed. These kinds of friendships are unselfish in nature, encouraging the growth and success of the other rather than viewing the other as a rival—in short, selfless friendships in Christlike humility.

Paul's humble love for Timothy was not in denial of his friend's imperfections. Uncharacteristically, Paul deviated from what he preached, feeling compelled to circumcise Timothy to better enable him to fit in with the Jews among whom he was working (Acts 16:3). What may have contributed to this was Paul's understanding that Timothy tended to be fearful in nature (see his admonishment of Timothy in 2 Tim. 1:7). While Paul was able to argue toe-to-toe with his enemies, Timothy might have felt intimidated to the point of it affecting his usefulness or even willingness to accompany Paul. And while Paul may have been comfortable living a celibate life, Timothy may not have been fully convinced it was what he wanted. For whatever reason, Paul warned Timothy to "flee the evil desires of youth and pursue righteousness, faith, love, and peace, along with those who call on the Lord out of a pure heart" (2 Tim. 2:22).

Paul had complete trust in Timothy because of his faith and proven ability, sending him to represent Paul when he could not come himself. He knew that his young protégé would see things as he did, would deal with the situations he found as Paul himself might, and would then bring a faithful, unblemished report back.

While Paul clearly depended upon the Lord for all things, he was also grateful that God had given him the gift of friendship with Timothy. That friendship did not divide Paul's loyalties. Rather, it further enriched his life and only confirmed and proved his love for Christ.

REFLECTION QUESTIONS

1. In thinking about the friendships you have or have had, which ones were beneficial and which ones were not? What was different about them?

2. How can friendships between two believers be more enriching than friendships between those who do not share in the fellowship of Christ?

15

PHILIPPIANS 2:25–30

Rome's armies were feared throughout the known world. One reason was they adapted one of the fighting styles of the Greeks. Most armies were little more than mobs of men who threw themselves wildly into battle or, at best, stood in long lines as they marched forward to the enemy. The Romans, however, were organized to fight side by side, forming phalanxes. Locking their shields together, they marched together toward the enemy, their shields extended and their swords at the ready. An enemy rarely faced a solitary Roman soldier in the initial battle. Instead they found soldiers who were not just fighting for themselves but their comrade beside them.

Paul spoke of Epaphroditus, who he calls his brother, fellow worker, and fellow soldier. In this great salvation war they were waging, Epaphroditus had proven himself to be a reliable companion at Paul's side. Beyond that, by using military terminology, Paul spoke of the urgency of the task before them, of the need for decisive action and a do-or-die spirit.

Epaphroditus had come to Paul from Philippi to minister to him and deliver a financial gift. Although we do not know the nature of the illness, along the way he had become very ill, so much so that it seemed almost certain he would die. We are told in Acts of the gift of healing Paul had so that even handkerchiefs he touched had a healing effect (see Acts 19:12). No doubt Paul prayed for his friend, but for reasons known only to God, Epaphroditus was not healed. Unlike what is sometimes preached today, miracles were not on demand but done in accordance with God's will.

The concern of the Philippians was such that when Epaphroditus heard of it he was "distressed." The Greek word for *distressed* speaks of intense emotion, used elsewhere to describe Jesus's agony in the Garden of Gethsemane (see Matt. 26:38; Mark 14:33). Epaphroditus was one of those souls who was more moved by the pain of others than anything he suffered. With communication so slow in those days, he knew that even when he recovered they would still think him ill and continue to be concerned for him.

Apparently Paul was sending his letter to the Philippians by the hand of Epaphroditus because he told them to "welcome him in the Lord." Paul cited Epaphroditus's willingness to risk his life for the work of Christ. In speaking of this, Paul used an interesting expression. The word *risk* in the original Greek was a gambling term. Dr. Witherington notes:

> The participle . . . which means "staked," "gambled," or "risked," may have been coined by Paul. The name Epaphroditus means "favorite of Aphrodite," the goddess of gambling, whose name one would invoke for luck when rolling the dice, but in the work of the Lord he staked his very life in order to fill up the lack of service the Philippians would not have been able to give otherwise.[1]

Paul considered Epaphroditus an example of the highest Christian values of selflessness and noble action. The danger he faced did not dissuade him from the goal before him. In a culture that promoted self-centeredness, Epaphroditus willingly went against that culture in order to serve Christ.

Chuck Swindoll in his book *Laugh Again*, quotes William Hendrickson's story of reckless risk for the sake of Christ.

> In the early church there were societies of men and women who called themselves *the parabolani*, that is, *the riskers and the gamblers*. They ministered to the sick and imprisoned, and they saw to it that, if at

all possible, martyrs and sometimes even enemies would receive an honorable burial. Thus in the city of Carthage during the great pestilence of AD 252 Cyprian, the bishop, showed remarkable courage. In self-sacrificing fidelity to his flock, and love even for his enemies, he took upon himself the care of the sick, and bade his congregation nurse them and bury the dead. What a contrast with the practice of the heathen who were throwing the corpses out of the plague-stricken city and were running away in terror.[2]

REFLECTION QUESTIONS

1. What do you make of God not healing Epaphroditus when, through Paul's hands, He had healed so many others?

2. What would be a risk for you to take for the gospel's sake? Are you willing? Why or why not?

PART 4

KNOWING
HIM

PHILIPPIANS 3:1–11

16

PHILIPPIANS 3:1–4

During the early 1500s, the Catholic Church was facing an economic crisis because of the expense of erecting the expansive St. Peter's Basilica in the Vatican. In order to generate more income and meet a demand among those concerned about the afterlife, the church promoted the sale of indulgences that were essentially gift certificates to reduce time in purgatory.

A young German priest, Martin Luther, was already conflicted about the teachings of the church, including the efficacy of some of the sacraments. But when the sale of indulgences started, it was too much. He drafted a document called the "Ninety-five Theses," nailing it to a church door in Wittenburg, Germany. With that act in 1517, the Protestant Reformation began. Discovering through prayer and research that grace was not for sale, nor the result of any kind of personal works, Luther came to believe the scriptural teaching that "the righteous will live by faith" (Rom. 1:17). It remains a key foundational principle among the Protestant churches.

Paul himself had dealt with this age-old problem of works being substituted for grace—just when the fledgling church had seemed to have been free of the idolatry of legalism that plagued the Jewish faith, the teaching of the Judaizers began to work its way in. Judaizers were Jewish believers who insisted that the Mosaic law in all its detail be practiced by Christian converts. The key battle was over the rite of circumcision, and to a lesser extent, the eating of kosher food as prescribed in the Pentateuch. Paul, supported by the apostles and church leaders, had decided that Gentile converts were not bound by the Jewish ceremonies (see Acts 15).

Even though the church leaders had absolved Gentile converts of the need to be circumcised as well as most restrictions on food, the Judaizers continued to teach otherwise. Most of the Gentile believers were totally new to the teaching of Scripture and so were understandably confused. Paul fought against the teaching of the Judaizers, arguing they were seeking to enslave the new believers in ceremonies that the Jewish people themselves found difficult to observe and, in fact, seldom fulfilled.

Some of Paul's strongest words against the Judaizer teachers are found in Philippians. "Watch out for those dogs, those evildoers, those mutilators of the flesh. For it is we who are the circumcision, we who serve God by his Spirit, who boast in Christ Jesus, and who put no confidence in the flesh" (vv. 2–3). Each phrase Paul used was like the lashing of a whip.

Paul called them dogs. While dogs are domesticated and beloved parts of many families today, the dogs during biblical times were largely untamed scavengers that ran in packs, often attacking passersby. Dogs were unclean animals to the Jews (see Lev. 11:27). They could not be eaten because they fed off the rotting corpses of other animals. To call a person a dog, then, was a sharp insult. Paul knew the Jews of his day commonly referred to Gentiles as dogs. Paul has turned the insult back on them.

He also called them "mutilators of the flesh," referring to the rite of circumcision. Fee points out, "The Greek word for circumcision is *peritome* ("to cut around"); *katatome*, used here, denotes "cutting to pieces," hence, "mutilate."[1] The words sounded similar when spoken but obviously had hugely different meanings. By calling circumcision mutilation, Paul accused the Judaizers of being like the heathen people the Jews conquered to take the Promised Land. Their worship often included horrific mutilations of animals and people as part of their worship, so these practices were forbidden among the Jews (see Lev. 21:5).

Contrary to the Judaizers' teaching, Paul insisted what mattered was the work of God in the heart. Outward observances had their place, and certainly a sacrament or ordinance can by its symbolism speak powerfully into the life of a believer—but the point was the life of the believer in relationship with God.

In and of themselves, symbols do not possess the ability to confer grace. Water is still water and bread is still bread. Paul wanted the Philippians to understand that the work of God was not dependent upon any rite or ceremony. Moreover, if there were any act that a person could do to receive saving merit, then the cross of Christ would be unnecessary. It is because we cannot earn our salvation or God's favor that grace is necessary. His grace is enough.

REFLECTION QUESTIONS

1. Should Christians follow Paul's example in insulting enemies of grace within the church? Why or why not?

2. What are the benefits of church ordinances or ceremonies? What are their limitations?

17

PHILIPPIANS 3:4–6

Richard DeHaan, in *Daily Bread*, shared the story of an instant cake mix that flopped. "The instructions said all you had to do was add water and bake. The company couldn't understand why it didn't sell — until their research discovered that the buying public felt uneasy about a mix that required only water. Apparently people thought it was too easy. So the company altered the formula and changed the directions to call for adding an egg to the mix in addition to the water. The idea worked and sales jumped dramatically."[1]

As Paul was dealing with the problem of salvation by works taught by the Judaizers, he decided to meet them on their own ground. It was important for Paul to establish to the Philippians and the church at large that the reason he forsook the Jewish faith was not because he was unqualified, that he failed, or that he was somehow mediocre in his pursuit of the kind of righteousness in which they believed.

Although it was distasteful to him, he laid out his pedigree. He began by stating that, even in infancy, he conformed to the law and was in good standing. "Circumcised on the eighth day, of the people of Israel, of the tribe of Benjamin, a Hebrew of Hebrews" (v. 5).

His circumcision on the eighth day proved that he was born into a devout Jewish family who followed the letter of the law regarding when a boy should be circumcised (Gen. 17:12).

Equally important was his reference to his lineage in the tribe of Benjamin. Many Jewish families lost track of their lineage during the time of the Babylonian captivity, but Paul's family had been careful to keep track of theirs to prove their ethnic purity. The tribe of Benjamin was noted because their forefather, Benjamin, was the only child of Jacob born in the Promised Land, the child of his favorite wife, Rachel. The first king of Israel, Saul, was from the tribe of Benjamin. Furthermore, when the nation of Israel separated into two nations, Israel and Judah, only the tribe of Benjamin sided with the tribe of Judah in seeking to be faithful to the Lord. Later it was the Benjamite, Mordecai, who was instrumental in the deliverance of the Jews as recorded in the book of Esther. To be a member of the tribe of Benjamin was to enjoy an especially honored place.

Now focusing on his practice as a Jew, Paul stated that he was a Hebrew of Hebrews. In this he meant that he was not just ethnically a Jew but had embraced all that it meant to be a Jew. The Jewish people preferred to call themselves Hebrews, so Paul recalled that special name in his account. Here Paul could cite his Hebrew parents who took him faithfully to the Hebrew synagogue, and who placed him in a highly honored Hebrew school where he sat at the feet of one of the great Hebrew scholars, Gamaliel. He spoke the Hebrew language, not just the common language of Aramaic. He read, not from the Greek translation of the Scriptures called the Septuagint, but from the original Hebrew that he used when citing Scriptures in his writing.

He then remarked that he was a Pharisee. The Pharisees' name meant "pure ones." They originally formed in the period between the testaments, during the Greek occupation of the Holy Land, as a people who set themselves aside to strictly observe Jewish practices and safeguard the Jewish religion from the encroachment of outside influences, particularly Greek. They were the fundamentalists of their day. It was their goal not only to observe what the law required, but to go above and beyond. While their goals were good, too many had become enamored with their self-righteousness by the time Jesus came. Nonetheless, to be a Pharisee was to dedicate oneself to the highest standards in one's practice of the Jewish faith. Pharisees were highly respected as a result.

Paul then spoke of his zeal in persecuting the church. At that time, he was determined to see those who converted to the Christian faith hunted down to recant their heresy or be killed. He wanted nothing more than to see the church driven to extinction. There is no evidence that in those days he saw his actions as anything less than totally righteous. He felt no guilt for defending his faith against what he saw at that time as the pollution of the heresy that was Christianity. He threw himself into it body and soul until stopped suddenly along the road to Damascus by the risen Christ (see Acts 9:1–31). Up until then he thought he was good and all he had done was good. He had no idea he was, in fact, attacking God Himself.

This is where Paul used to be. He had gone much further than the Judaizers ever had. They had nothing on him. Unlike them, however, he was made to realize the idolatry of his lost condition.

REFLECTION QUESTIONS

1. What advantages or disadvantages can there be with families who have a long history as believers?

2. Did Paul's allegiance to the Jewish faith work for or against him? Why?

18

PHILIPPIANS 3:7–8

"The Prince Albert Coat" aired originally on May 10, 1957, as part of the *Adventures of Superman* series. It told the story of a young boy who wanted to help a charity drive by giving his great-grandfather's coat. The problem was that the coat had sewn into its lining ten thousand dollars, the man's life savings. Some criminals found out about the fortune and stole the coat. Through the help of the superhero, the coat eventually was recovered, but when it was opened, in the lining was Confederate money. What the boy had seen as so very valuable was worthless.

In the previous verses Paul defended himself against his critics by proving he was more Jewish than most of his accusers. This message of Paul hammered mercilessly against the teaching of the Judaizers. He had been born and had accomplished what they all longed for. Having laid that out, he gave his valuation of what the supposed faith advantages all meant to him. "I consider everything a loss because of the surpassing worth of knowing Christ Jesus my Lord, for whose sake I have lost all things. I consider them garbage, that I may gain Christ" (v. 8).

The language Paul used to describe his past accomplishments was strong and extreme. He used accounting terms, setting gain against loss. In doing so, the word for *gain* was plural while the word for *loss* was singular. By doing this he showed that those gains for which he had so long labored and dedicated himself were gone in a moment. When he spoke of all the past being lost, he was saying that it was not only gone but it was never to be touched again. There was no door open, no bridge to cross over to the other side again. Paul knew that the old affections could not be salvaged, nor could he pull back part of the sacrifice from the altar. Remembering Lot's wife's fatal longing look (see Gen. 19:26), Paul knew he must never cast a wishful glance backwards.

He went even further to say that the works of the past were garbage. Dr. J. B. Lightfoot has helpfully described the shades of meaning to the Greek word *skybala* that the NIV translates as "garbage":

1. "Excrement," the portion of food rejected by the body as not possessing any nutritive qualities. This sense is frequent in medical writers.

2. "The refuse or leavings of a feast," the food thrown away from the table. The Judaizers spoke of themselves as banqueters seated at the Father's table, of Gentile Christians as dogs greedily snatching up the refuse meat which fell from there. St. Paul reversed the image. The Judaizers [were] themselves "dogs" (see Phil. 3:2); the meats served to the sons of God [were] spiritual meats; the ordinances, which the formalists value[d] so highly, [were] the mere refuse of the feast.[1]

Paul realized that no matter how "good" everything might have seemed, it was actually harmful because it had stood in the way of his knowing Christ as Savior. The believer joins Paul in this recognition. Sometimes we work or long for things that, once gained, actually work against us because they keep us from Christ. An example of how this works could be found with the king of Thailand, who by law had to be a Buddhist. If he did not remain Buddhist, he must abdicate. So in spite of the wealth, honor, and power in his position as king, these things became a road-block to his salvation in Christ. This is an extreme example. For most people it is far, far less that keeps them from Christ. The supposed good then is sin in that it separates us from God (the definition of sin).

Paul has replaced all of this with "the surpassing worth of knowing Christ Jesus my Lord . . . that I may gain

Christ" (v. 8). It is not just that the former things were so much clutter and garbage, but that their true value, or rather their poverty, became apparent when Jesus Christ came into view.

Most little girls love plastic jewelry with gaudy fake gems, but when compared to a diamond ring in a gold setting, their true value becomes obvious. So also when Christ comes and we know Him, the old things look cheap and useless. The excellence of Christ puts everything into its proper place and shows its true worth.

REFLECTION QUESTIONS

1. Has there been anything in your life that you longed to have, but when you got it, you wished you hadn't?

2. What things from our past can be salvaged and what things should be treated as garbage?

19

PHILIPPIANS 3:9

In 2009, a developer in Rhode Island hired an engineering firm to survey beachfront land on which he wanted to build a 2-million-dollar home which, when completed, he planned to put on the market. Everything checked out and the house went up without any problems. A buyer was found, but when he had an independent engineer check things out, it was discovered that the home was built on the wrong land owned by a park. In spite of the developer's pleading, the court ruled in favor of the park, telling the developer that he would have to move it or tear it down.[1]

Paul established in the earlier verses that he had previously built his life in the wrong place. That discovery came at the precise moment he found Christ as Savior.

Paul described the new placement of his life as being "found in Him." This is far more than an intellectual belief in the doctrinal truth that Christ came through the incarnation, was crucified, and rose again for our salvation. That is part of it. But it is a heart knowledge that causes the life to pivot from one direction and head in another. Being found in Christ meant that Paul was not presenting himself any longer as a good person or a Hebrew of Hebrews, but rather clothing himself in the righteousness of Christ.

When he stands before God at the end of his life, it will not be with a long list of accomplishments or a recitation of his good works. Imagine the question being asked, "By what right do you enter heaven?" Paul would reply, "By the righteousness of Christ." Nothing more and certainly nothing less.

The phrase "in Christ" or similar wording is sprinkled throughout Paul's writing. It is the beautiful expression of a living, abiding, and intimate fellowship with the Savior that nourishes, protects, cleanses, and equips the child of God. It represents all our innate inadequacies and shortcomings being met with the sufficiency of our Lord. As an embryo in the mother is fed, warmed, protected, and given all that is needed to grow, so we who are in Christ find our present protection and future provision in this relationship with Him.

Paul spoke of "not having a righteousness of my own that comes from the law, but that which is through faith in Christ" (v. 9). Righteousness suggests a legal standing before God, when we are justified through the work of the Savior on our behalf. But it is more than that. It speaks of a restoration of our right relationship with God. The offenses that separated us from Him are now as far as the east is from the west. The stains of sin have been washed away in the blood of Christ. And with that, He claims us as His children and we claim Him as our Lord.

That restoration of relationship is not only with God but with other people as well. The social aspect of salvation is part and parcel of what it means to be a Christian. The closer we grow to the Lord, the more concerned we are with relationships with others. As His life continues to grow within us, it is not enough for our salvation to be assured. We are concerned about the lost world around us. It is more than a mental assent that something should be done; it is the motivation to be up and doing. Relationship is more than a concept, it is a reality because of the work of Christ's righteousness in us.

All this is beautifully expressed in a poem entitled, "My Master" that is included in Chuck Swindoll's book *Laugh Again*.

I had walked life's path with an easy tread,
Had followed where comfort and pleasure led;
And then by chance in a quiet place—
I met my Master face to face.

With station and rank and wealth for goal,
Much thought for body but none for soul,
I had entered to win this life's mad race—
When I met my Master face to face.

I had built my castles, reared them high,
Till their towers had pierced the blue of the sky;
I had sworn to rule with an iron mace—
When I met my Master face to face.

I met Him and knew Him, and blushed to see
That His eyes full of sorrow were fixed on me;
And I faltered, and fell at His feet that day
While my castles vanished and melted away.

Melted and vanished; and in their place
I saw naught else but my Master's face;
And I cried aloud: "Oh, make me meet
To follow the marks of Thy wounded feet."

My thought is now for the souls of men;
I have lost my life to find it again
Ever since alone in that holy place
My Master and I stood face to face.[2]

REFLECTION QUESTIONS

1. How would you describe being found in Christ to someone who is not a Christian?

2. In what way does your faith in Christ affect your relationships?

20

PHILIPPIANS 3:10–11

Having laid out the foundation for his relationship with Christ, Paul then said, "I want to know [Him]" (v.10). The word used for *know* in Greek has a corresponding identical meaning in Hebrew. The word represents the most personal and thorough knowledge. In Genesis, it referred to the sexual union between a man and a woman, that most intimately loving of human acts. Without the sexual overtones, Paul said he wanted to know Christ as intimately as a husband and wife know each other or a mother knows her child. It is not just to have a collection of facts. It is to know the motives, the priorities, what hurts and what helps another person, what makes him or her happy or sad.

Paul understood the more he knew Christ, the greater his devotion to Him would be. Paul concluded that every important fact in the world led to Christ. Creation spoke of Him. The rituals of Jewish religion were patterns of His work. The temple with its furnishings all spoke of Him. The prophets saw Him over the ruin of the world around them. The history of the world itself, even the truths that survived through the distortions of other religions, spoke of Christ. He learned of Him from all legitimate teachings, and learned the significance and proper place of all these things by knowing Christ.

So Christ is made known to us by our worship, by the Word of God, by prayer. He is known by our experience of Him. We can describe the sweetness of honey and tell of its chemical makeup, but it can only be truly known by tasting it. Painted fires do not burn, and just looking at water will not wash dirty hands. It is only in experiencing the real thing that anything is accomplished. Christ must be known experientially or He is not known at all.

Paul then said that he wanted to know the "power of his resurrection" (v. 10). This great central truth for all of Christianity, this foundational fact upon which all Christian belief and teaching pivots, must never be ignored or given a mere token nod. It was not so for the early Christians. Even a cursory reading of the New Testament and the early church fathers revealed that they found this one fact was more than important. They hardly could keep themselves from speaking about it. The thrill of it leaped from the pages as certainly as the stone rolled away on that resurrection morning.

The power of the resurrection fooled the disciples. They were sure the power arrived on that Palm Sunday when Jesus entered Jerusalem. No king would have been welcomed with greater enthusiasm. As conquering heroes, the disciples walked in the wake of Christ's train, sure (they must have thought) to be the advisors in the new kingdom being born on this day.

And the common wisdom might have been, if not in the victory parade, then the betrayal or even the crucifixion would surely be the next place for power to be displayed. Pilate and the Roman soldiers should have faded away like dew before the morning sun. The Jewish leaders who opposed Christ should have run for their lives like refugees ahead of a ruthless army. But no such thing came to be. Perhaps the mocking tones of those surrounding the cross reflected the dashed hopes among the disciples: "Those who passed by hurled insults at him, shaking their heads and saying, 'You who are going to destroy the temple and build it in three days, save Yourself! Come down from the cross, if you are the Son of God'" (Matt. 27:39–40).

What better display of power could there be than ripping one's hands and feet from the cross and coming down in power to banish all enemies? But Jesus stayed.

And in staying He died, with the anticlimax of His limp body being borne away by a handful of grief-stricken women.

Power would come when every human possibility was fully accounted for and eliminated. Power would flash in a lightless tomb, spreading like the rays of the rising sun.

It is the glorious power of that Easter morning that Paul wanted to know. Why? Because there was no power greater. Why? Because there was no power more transforming. Why? Because when Christ arose, He reached out His hand to take you and me up with Him.

Finally, Paul spoke of wanting to intimately know "participation in his sufferings," what some versions translate as the *fellowship* of his sufferings (v. 10). Paul knew this meant understanding pain at a deeper level than ever before fathomed. Christ's suffering also was for different reasons than what is the common lot of humanity.

Christ's suffering was intended to happen. The natural response to pain is to avoid it or end it as quickly as possible. Touch your finger to a hot stove. Your reaction is to get away from the stove and then to find a way to make your finger stop hurting.

There are times when we undergo a painful experience intentionally, but it is usually in order to accomplish a self-benefiting end. A person submits to surgery not because he relishes having himself cut open, but because the suffering in surgery is the price to be paid to prevent a worse calamity.

Not so for Jesus. When He chose to suffer, it was His intention to undergo it, to feel the full force of pain in the moments of His betrayal, humiliation, and crucifixion. He intended to do it not because it would meet any good end for Himself, but so it would accomplish His intended purposes for us. Had He not come to earth to live, suffer, and die, the galaxies would have continued to spin, the seasons would still follow one after another, and the angels would go on about their heavenly services, but the people of this world would remain hopelessly lost in sin. Jesus's suffering was for our sake.

Paul knew he could not share the sufferings of Christ in their intensity. Only the Son of God could take onto Himself the sins of the world, suffer the consequence of separation from the Father, and yet remain the only pure soul amid the swamp of sin that earth had become. Only Christ could bear it, but in doing so, he was afflicted by it through and through.

Paul specified that he wanted to share in the "fellowship" of His suffering. The word *fellowship* in the original language is the same one used for the partnership Peter and Andrew had in their fishing businesses. As Jesus's partners, we fall in behind Him while He plows the way ahead. We walk in the footsteps of bleeding feet; we carry our cross in His way with the stains of nail-scarred hands; we bend our head with Him beneath the press of thorns on His head.

And we do this intentionally. The criminal had his cross sentenced to him and would escape it if he could have. But the follower of Christ purposely takes up his cross to follow Jesus.

Paul would seek a crown, yes. But he would do so as did his Master. Through the cross. Through the fellowship of suffering.

REFLECTION QUESTIONS

1. How do you seek to know Christ more intimately?
2. How can you share in the sufferings of Christ?

PART 5

WHAT'S BECOMING
OF US?

PHILIPPIANS 3:12–21

21

PHILIPPIANS 3:12

C. S. Lewis, although raised to attend church and pray, declared himself an atheist in his college years. He was troubled by both the existence of evil and what he perceived to be the meaninglessness of life. Speaking of this time, he said, "Nearly all I loved I believed to be imaginary; nearly all that I believed to be real, I thought grim and meaningless."[1] Although he hoped for better things, he felt reality was dark and hopeless. Drawn to Christian authors, particularly G.K. Chesterton, he was surprised by the growing interest he was having in the Christian faith. As he read, his objections to Christianity began to fade away.

While riding a bus in Oxford, Lewis felt he was, as he said it, "holding something at bay, or shutting something out." He could either open the door or let it stay shut, but to open the door "meant the incalculable." He finally submitted himself to God, the most "dejected and reluctant convert" in all England. This belief in God happened in 1929, but it was not until 1931 that he surrendered himself to Christ. From the time of his conversion in 1931, Lewis sought to know more and more about his newfound Lord. Although still writing about medieval literature while serving as a professor at Oxford, he also turned his considerable writing talent and sharp mind to Christian fantasy, for example, *The Chronicles of Narnia*, and apologetics, *Mere Christianity*, his most well-known non-fiction work. His British Broadcasting Corporation radio addresses were legendary while his books continued to influence Christians and non-believers alike, generations after his death.

C.S. Lewis's experience somewhat mirrored Paul's. Although Paul was not an atheist, his abhorrence to Christianity rivaled Lewis's. In Philippians, he carefully laid out his previous status and his view of those former days. He spoke about his change of priorities from disdaining Christ to seeking above all else to "know Him," from inflicting suffering on believers to seeking "participation in his sufferings" (3:10).

Paul qualified, "Not that I have already obtained all this" (v. 12). The church father Theodoret paraphrased Paul's perspective: "'It was he who first caught me in the net,' said Paul in effect, 'for I was fleeing him and was turned well away. He caught me as I fled. But now I in turn am the pursuer in my desire to catching him, that I may not be a disappointment to his saving work."[3] Paul, who ran away, was now running toward the Lord he had spurned.

Paul then talked about one side of a Christian paradox. Christian perfection remains a highly controversial subject, mostly because those who decry it view it from a very narrow perspective. The Christian who lives a holy life dedicated to perfectly loving God and neighbors is in one most important way "perfect" or complete. And yet in another way his or her life remains "imperfect" or still incomplete. We can be perfect in the sense we have submitted everything we know to the Lord's control, that He has become the supreme ruler of our lives. We desire Him above any sin or temptation that might lure us away. In God's eyes, that is a perfect heart as spoken of throughout Scripture.

Enjoying this kind of perfection, however, hardly means we are a finished product. While I may in this moment open my heart fully to the Holy Spirit, asking Him to reveal any harbored, sinful attitude or action contrary to His will, He may show me something or nothing at all. The Lord knows what we can take, and to reveal to us all at once all of our imperfections and areas that need growth might overwhelm us. As we are ready, He leads us along to new truth and deeper understanding until when the problem area is brought to our attention, we can then seek His help in dealing with whatever it is.

Along with this is the reality that we change as we enter and then go through different stages of life. The dimension of grace needed for a new parent is different than the dimension of grace needed as a person faces the end of his or her life. What we need to know is shown to us at the point of our need. Because we continue to grow as people and continue to expand in our roles and responsibilities, we continue to need to grow spiritually. So even while living a holy life with perfect hearts, we can find we are not perfectly finished or fitted for everything. The Holy Spirit works with our yielded will so He can accomplish His work. With Paul, we can honestly say we have not already arrived at our goal of perfection.

Like Paul, we "press on to take hold of that for which Christ Jesus took hold of [us]." We understand that today's surrender is not the last one, that yesterday's breakthrough, while wonderful, is not the end of the battles ahead of us. Our hope is that we can take hold of Christ, because He who leads us holds us as well. We are safe where He leads, only in danger if we refuse to follow.

REFLECTION QUESTIONS

1. Have you ever tried to run from God? What brought you back?

2. How is it for you to live in the tension between perfect and imperfect?

22

PHILIPPIANS 3:13–14

The 1936 Olympic games were held in Berlin, the premiere city of what was then Nazi Germany. Adolf Hitler yearned for the games to prove to the world the strength of Germany as well as the superiority of what he termed the "pure Aryan race." The Nazis' disdain for other races, while particularly focused on Jews, also included many people of other races. The times were tense as Hitler was openly arming his nation for the war that would engulf the world three years later. At this point, Hitler wanted to win the propaganda war with the Olympic games as his showpiece.

Enter Jesse Owens, an African American and supremely skilled runner. Although he was a representative of the United States (US), his skin color subjected him to discrimination before and after the games in his home country. Many white supremacists in the US were embarrassed that a

Black man was America's representative. Knowing of this as well as the antipathy of the Nazis, Owens refused to be distracted and in dazzling fashion won gold medals in the one-hundred meter, two-hundred meter, long jump, and four by one-hundred meter relay. If anyone could have blamed defeat on the distractions around him, it would have been Jesse Owens. But he kept his eye on the prize and ran to victory.

Paul spoke of that very same idea with the metaphor of a spiritual race. In describing how he viewed his spiritual journey, he first said that he was "forgetting what [was] behind" (v. 13). Chuck Swindoll commenting on this forgetting, said it like this.

> The original word Paul used when he wrote, "forgetting what lies behind," was a Greek term that meant fully forgetting, *completely* forgetting. Actually, it was an ancient athletic term used of a runner who outran another in the same race: Once he got into the lead, he would never turn and look back; he would forget about the other runner.[1]

While we cannot totally forget our past, nor is it wise to do so, the forgetting spoken of here is about putting thoughts out of the mind—a refusal to dwell on the past. There are people who are obsessed with what could or should have happened, often blaming others for their poor station in life or lack of success. How much better their life would be if they'd commit their ways to the Lord and chose, as Paul, to forget everything but pursuing Christ! Instead Paul described his "straining toward what is ahead" (v. 13). He would not be distracted by side issues nor would he be burdened with the weight of ceremonies or attitudes that slowed his progress.

A Greek fable tells of two runners preparing for a race. One knew he had no chance of winning because he was not as fast as his competitor. He surprised the other runner when he showed up at the starting line with five golden apples. Bolting out into the lead, as he ran and could feel the other runner getting close, he would drop an apple. As he expected, the runner would stop to pick it up. Each time he sensed the other runner, he dropped another apple. As he did so, he relieved himself of the weight he was carrying while the other racer lost distance and took on the extra weight of the apples. The slow runner won because the faster runner had his mind on something other than the race. Paul said he was straining, focusing on what was ahead, and he would not allow himself to be turned aside.

He noted that "one thing" was on his mind. The English rendering is not strong enough. Actually, it should emphasize "*but* one thing," at the exclusion of everything else. That single-minded focus was propelling him forward.

Although he sat in prison, likely chained, he was free to run the race of Christ totally focused.

Where was Paul going? "I press on toward the goal to win the prize for which God has called me heavenward in Christ Jesus" (v. 14). He was headed for the reward that was his for eternity. It is the tendency in our time to not talk too much about heaven or the reward that awaits the believer except, perhaps, at funerals. While we should be relevant to the time in which we live, we need to remember that our life here on earth is like the opening credits of a movie—the real story follows. Paul knew that, and as he got closer to the end of his life, he was energized by what was awaiting him. Death for him was not going to be some sad occasion or approached with armfuls of regret. It was the ribbon that was to be broken as he crossed the finish line. Then, in a glory we could not comprehend, he would receive his reward.

Flemming explains, "The picture would be of the presiding judge calling up the victor at the race's end to receive a prize, usually a laurel."[2] The promise to the believer is what awaits us: the flush of victory and the commendation of our Lord. And unlike earthly races where there is but one victor, we all can cross the finish line in victory as we pursue the upward call of God in Christ Jesus.

REFLECTION QUESTIONS

1. What should you forget and what should you remember?

2. When you think of entering heaven, what do you think it will be like? How can your life either prepare you or hinder you in winning the race?

23

PHILIPPIANS 3:15–17

When I have had the opportunity to teach, I often encounter people with different views on the subject at hand. After I discuss a point with them, we explore the validity of each other's point, then I like to jokingly say, "Of course, you are entitled to your own opinion—if you don't mind being wrong." There is a bit of that in this passage as Paul continued to address his Philippian friends.

The NIV weakens the strength of the passage by using the word *mature* instead of the more correct rendering of *perfect* as is found in a number of other translations. Some compromise and use a hybrid, *perfectly mature*, whatever that may mean. It is clear that it is easier in the present to speak of maturity rather than perfection, but as we previously discussed, the perfection spoken of in relation to the believer is not the idea of someone who is absolutely perfect, with no room for improvement. It is rather the idea of complete and whole. Flemming points out that in the Septuagint, the word *perfect* means "those whose hearts are wholly devoted to God."[1]

Maturity is certainly an important and desirable trait, especially in spiritual matters, but it lacks the strength Paul apparently meant to convey in choosing the word he did. While maturity speaks of experience and the wisdom gained through study and reflection, the full devotion and total commitment found in the word *perfect* are the grounds on which Paul spoke to the Philippians. Maturity is a part of biblical perfection, but the reverse is not necessarily so.

There was a slight edge in Paul's statement that said, "And if on some point you think differently, that too God will make clear to you" (v. 15). Paul was not talking so much about the way people expressed themselves. What he was trying to convey was while there may be flexibility in some things, there are others that are non-negotiable. In a way he was saying, "If you love the Lord fully and have grown in your faith, you will reach these same conclusions." He was arguing that the Spirit of God will not lead to thoughts that contradict Scripture or the wisdom of the Christian faith. Although postmodernism dismisses the notion of absolute truth, it doesn't mean that absolute truth fails to exist. There are certainly areas of faith that are not clear cut and that are subject to some individual interpretation. Believers can explore those areas even if it vexed Paul a bit.

His answer was to encourage believers to follow his example. While that sounds conceited to our modern minds, it was a common practice in ancient times for philosophers and teachers to place themselves before their students as examples of their teaching. As we think about it, whenever we give advice to another person by speaking of lessons we have learned, or telling of how we handled this or that, we are essentially saying, "Imitate me." Perhaps we aren't putting it as bluntly as Paul said it here, but it delivers the same message.

Paul was in good standing in offering himself as an example of Christlike humility. In his second letter to the Corinthians, when being maligned by those who tried to dilute his influence, he answered with an incredible rendition of the selfless love he had been living out by the power of and love for Christ and for those neighbors whom God placed in his path:

> I have worked much harder, been in prison more frequently, been flogged more severely, and been exposed to death again and again. Five times I received from the Jews the forty lashes minus one. Three times I was beaten with rods, once I was pelted with stones, three times I was shipwrecked,

I spent a night and a day in the open sea, I have been constantly on the move. I have been in danger from rivers, in danger from bandits, in danger from my fellow Jews, in danger from Gentiles; in danger in the city, in danger in the country, in danger at sea; and in danger from false believers. I have labored and toiled and have often gone without sleep; I have known hunger and thirst and have often gone without food; I have been cold and naked. Besides everything else, I face daily the pressure of my concern for all the churches (2 Cor. 11:23–28).

On the positive side, Paul's letters became and have remained incredibly helpful in understanding and applying the Christian faith. Obviously God the Holy Spirit found a quick and ready mind to inspire to write the various letters that make up more than half the books of our New Testament. Literally it can be said that Paul had every right to refer to himself as an example since he had experienced firsthand the deep joy of participating in the fellowship of Christ's suffering for the sake of others.

REFLECTION QUESTIONS

1. How do you deal with people who view matters of faith differently than you?

2. Could you say to someone, "Follow my example"? Why or why not?

24

PHILIPPIANS 3:18–19

In the original preface to C. S. Lewis's classic *The Screwtape Letters*, he aptly characterized the primary, terrible characteristic of hell's population—a self-consuming self-centeredness that was disturbingly reminiscent of worldly mind-sets prevalent here and now:

[Hell is] an official society held together entirely by fear and greed. On the surface, manners are normally suave. Rudeness to one's superiors would obviously be suicidal; rudeness to one's equals might put them on their guard before you were ready to spring your mine. For of course "Dog eat dog" is the principle of the whole organization. Everyone wishes everyone else's discrediting, demotion, and ruin; everyone is an expert in the confidential report, the pretended alliance, the stab in the back. Over all this their good manners, their expressions of grave respect, their "tributes" to one another's invaluable services form a thin crust. Every now and then it gets punctured, and the scalding lava of their hatred spurts out.[1]

In contrast to his own model of self-sacrificing humility, Paul cautioned against the "many [who] live as enemies of the cross of Christ" (v. 18). These are the proud occupants of hell on earth—they are ruled by the anti-humility spirit of self-centeredness and self-promotion. Far from the mind-set of Jesus Christ that would lower oneself for the sake of others (even to the point of dying so painfully on a cross), the person whose "mind is set on earthly things" (v. 19) is about lifting self above all others. This is the survival-of-the-fittest mind-set, always looking out for number one. The way of the world is about putting up crosses for others to bear; the furthest thing from their minds is taking any up for themselves. Any capacity for love or relationship they might have is notoriously only as deep as their own shallow self—thus "their god is [nothing more than] their stomach" (v. 19).

If Paul had the Judaizers in mind, his irony was thick here. The reference to their god being their belly could likewise have implied their obsessively legalistic lording over others through dietary laws. No doubt they were scandalized when they saw the Gentile Christians freely eating pork or meat that was not kosher.

The other reference of "their glory is in their shame" (v. 19) could very well be a reference to their private parts. With the insistence that all Gentile men be circumcised, the Judaizers obsessively were making reference to male anatomy, something ordinarily rarely spoken about publicly in Jewish circles. That which should have been private, or handled with healthy modesty, was something they gloried in. It was almost like they were saying, "I am one of God's chosen. Come view my privates." Unbelievable.

There is also thought that some of these who were enemies were those who claimed to be Christians yet lived grossly immoral lives. The *Beacon Commentary* notes that often in ancient literature the belly refers to the womb.[2] It is not surprising that with the large influx of Gentiles into the church there would be some who came along who brought with them the practices of their heathen religions. Many of these involved temple prostitutes or orgies that were part of their so-called worship.

Syncretism, the attempt to combine different religions, was common among first-generation believers, as it is even to this day. The suggestion that self-serving immorality was part of worship would not have sounded out of line to the new convert who may have come from religions that practiced it. But once involved, it was difficult to extricate them from the deviant behavior, especially if a respected person was telling him or her it was all right. Paul insisted on the biblical standard of sexual purity in marriage—intimacy with a spouse rather than self-gratification without committed love for another.

What church father John Chrysostom said in the fourth century is relevant for us today: "Your body is given to you that you may rule it, not so that you may have it as a mistress."[3] We need to be careful. Obviously there can be good pleasure in eating, and looking nice is not bad. Exercise is beneficial. But when any of these becomes a selfish obsession that makes it the primary motivator in life, it is on par with the enemies of the cross that Paul addressed.

There should be alarm as well about any symptoms of loose morality that can still be as prevalent in the church as out. The telling attitude is notoriously, "If I don't feel bad, it can't be wrong," or even worse, "It's what makes me happy." Such should be obviously antithetical to the humble mind-set of Christ, whose concern is not about serving one's own interests. The Bible makes no such allowances for a so-called faith that prioritizes narcissism or self-serving interests.

How will these people end up? "Their destiny is destruction" (v. 19). Paul left no doubt of the end result of this kind of lifestyle—the self-destructive hell they lived now on earth was only a foreshadowing of their misery in eternity. When people choose self-interest over God's will, they cut themselves off from their only hope of salvation. Contrast that with previous verses where Paul spoke of the goal set before him. As Psalm 1 says so succinctly, "For the Lord watches over the way of the righteous, but the way of the wicked leads to destruction" (v. 6). Self-serving is nothing other than self-destruction.

REFLECTION QUESTIONS

1. How can essential and good things progress to the place where they are a hindrance to faith?

2. Describe ways your body can serve as the temple of the Holy Spirit. Is your body helping or hindering you?

25

PHILIPPIANS 3:20–21

When my family and I lived overseas, we had to have permission from the country's government that allowed us to live and work there. Papers were issued to us that we were to carry in case we needed to prove we were legally admitted. Even though we were immersed in the country, we remained citizens of the United States of America. Although far from home, we had every right and privilege as any other American citizen. We also knew that if certain needs arose, we could call upon the government of the United States to come to our aid. We also knew at some point we would leave to return to our home country. Although we lived there, our citizenship was somewhere else.

The first century church was increasingly a melting pot of nationalities, races, and ages. In the congregations there were a mixture of the rich and poor, the cultured and barbaric.

The master might find himself taught by his slave while the former prostitute broke bread with the one steeped in religious tradition. Though their backgrounds varied widely, they found common ground at the feet of Christ. Each would go out, plunged into cultures that neither understood nor liked them. But they gathered back together where their voices blended in songs to the Savior and they fed upon the Word as they moved forward in their faith.

In a hostile environment, they formed what was a colony of fellow citizens of heaven. Here there was the beginning of eternal life, and these believers among whom they sat and worshiped were their countrymen in the kingdom of God. No Greek or Jew, or barbarian or foreigner. Christ united them as fellow citizens. The world had never seen this before. The Roman Empire began to see in this a growing threat as the church drew people of all kinds together, something that the Roman Empire hoped to do but never accomplished. It was a great wonder, and it still is.

We are united by our hope of the return of Christ and His reclamation of the earth. Satan is called the god of this age (see 2 Cor. 4:3–4), but in reality he is a squatter. God holds the title deed to this earth. When Christ returns, the squatter will be swept away, and our Lord will once again reclaim what is His. Even as He comes to reclaim the earth, He will allow us to reclaim our bodies.

The Greeks believed that the soul would shed the body much as a snake sheds its skin. Other religions have taught that the body is like a suit of clothes we wear out, and then through reincarnation we are fitted with a new one for a time. But the Bible knows nothing of these concepts. The artificial separation of the physical from the spiritual is not a Christian belief. God created us as integrated units. The body is more than a vehicle or vessel for the soul because the two are unified. Evidence of this comes when we are sick. Who feels like shouting praises when they have the flu? The body most decidedly affects the spirit. On the other hand, when we are unwell we find that our praise and labors for the Lord can lift us so we feel physically better. The body and soul are organically linked.

Paul said Jesus "by the power that enables him to bring everything under his control, will transform our lowly bodies so that they will be like his glorious body" (v. 21). This is a startling declaration. These bodies, which serve us so well one minute only to betray us the next, will finally become what they were always meant to be, had our first parents not brought sin into the world. The prototype of what we can expect is found in Christ Himself in His resurrection body, "Like his glorious body," (v. 21) Paul said. Dr. Witherington succinctly summarized, "Christ's history is the believer's destiny."[1]

The *Beacon Bible Commentary* notes further that the new outward appearance of the glorified body will be fashioned and formed in ways "appropriate to its inner spiritual character."[2] Apparently we will be recognizable somehow in our physical form, but the inner us will now supplement that appearance in some way. We see people of whom we say, "She is the picture of love." Perhaps that is a foretaste of life in the kingdom. We will be on the outside what we are on the inside. All we are becoming now in Christ is the DNA of our resurrection bodies.

REFLECTION QUESTIONS

1. If we take seriously the idea that our citizenship is in heaven, how does that change what we are doing now?

2. Imagine your glorified body that reflects the condition of your soul as well. What will you look like?

PART 6

ABASED
AND ABOUNDING

PHILIPPIANS 4:1–23

26

PHILIPPIANS 4:1–3

A few years ago I was talking to my superior about some frustrations I was having with other members of the staff. He acknowledged that there were some problems but very gently reminded me, "We are swimming in a small pool. We are bound to bump into each other from time to time." I forget what I complained about, but have often thought about his wisdom.

Before dealing with dissension, Paul called upon the believers to "stand firm in the Lord" (v. 1). Richard R. Melick, Jr. noted that "Roman armies were known for standing unmoved against the enemy. The church was to stand in the same way."[1] Standing together means being unified in purpose and with healthy dependence upon each other. We would say now that he expected them to work as a team.

Throughout his letter to the Philippians, Paul returned, to the issue of disunity. In this passage, he singled out two women whose differences must have been so sharp as to merit special mention. Paul did not need to demonstrate his authority but took a different tack, saying, "I plead" (v. 2). No doubt he had great affection and appreciation for both women. Their dispute was not something to attack but instead caused him grief. In Philippi as now, we sometimes find ourselves bystanders of disputes, and if not drawn in by one faction or another, just longing for the parties involved to settle their differences with a humble spirit of forgiveness.

Paul requested an unnamed person to mediate, calling him or her "my true companion." The King James Version translates this as *yokefellow*, which is a beautiful picture of someone sharing closely alongside us, working as hard as two oxen yoked together. In this Paul was saying that this person was one he treated as an equal, a true companion whose reliability was well known.

If Paul were there, he would have mediated the dispute, but since he could not, this trusted colleague was called upon to act in his stead. Since the women apparently could not or chose not to work it through on their own, a gentle hand to guide them was what was needed. As any who have tried to insert themselves into a disagreement will know, this is no easy task. Paul's confidence in his friend must have been very high to put before that person such a difficult task.

It is important to notice the women's place of leadership in the church. Chrysostom noted, "These women seem to me to be the chief of the Church which was there."[2] There is no indication from Scripture that women were considered inferior in any way; in fact, they were respected leaders. The Holy Spirit does not discriminate as to whom He gifts, and certainly not because of gender.

The Salvation Army was the first denomination to declare women were equals in ministry with men. There is little doubt that The Salvation Army could not have reached as many with the gospel without the full engagement of women with their gifting in leadership in its global outreach. Catherine Booth, dubbed the mother of The Salvation Army, wrote concerning women in ministry:

If she has the necessary gifts, and feels herself called by the Spirit to preach, there is not a single word in the whole Book of God to restrain her, but many, very many to urge and encourage her. God says she shall do so, and Paul prescribed the manner in which she shall do it, and Phebe, Junia, Phillip's four daughters, and many other women actually did preach and speak in the primitive churches. If this had not been the case, there would have been less freedom under the new than under the old dispensation.[3]

Despite many passages popularly cited by other spectrums of Christianity, most are about the marriage relationship, not church leadership dynamics. And on those few occasions Paul did speak to women's roles in churches, he clearly expressed his own preference in dealing with the difficult realities of cultural norms at that time. For instance, despite the favorite (though unique) reference cited by those opposed to ordination of women in 1 Timothy, it is clear from this passage in Philippians and several others that there were several scenarios in which Paul did indeed "permit a woman to teach or to assume authority over a man" (2:12).

Though a believer, in reality, Paul taught that in Christ there was "neither male nor female" (Gal. 3:28), Paul was working in a human culture and religious tradition that was stiff necked and patriarchal. As did Jesus himself, Paul had to condescend and deal with cultural injustices as they were, be they slavery or misogyny.

Paul then spoke not only about women but about Clement and others who had shared in the work of the gospel. He noted that their names were written in the "Book of Life" (v. 3). The idea of a registration book was familiar to the ancient people. The Bible tells of such a registry for the Jewish people (see Ps. 69:28; Isa. 4:3). At the death of a prominent person, it was the practice to read out their name for a praiseworthy life, an honor that was cherished.

The Philippians whose names were found in the Book of Life had the assurance of salvation that comes with faith in Christ. These who had been so faithful could expect the honor and peace that comes from knowing they had a place in the kingdom.

REFLECTION QUESTIONS

1. What is the best strategy for dealing with disputes in the church?

2. What qualifies a person for ministry? Should gender be an issue?

27

PHILIPPIANS 4:4–7

Prisons in Paul's day were not places to punish people as they are now. They most often served as holding places for those awaiting execution or transfer. As such, they were filthy, full of disease, and dimly lit. Food rations were poor and wholly inadequate. There was no concern about conditions being overcrowded or any violence that might occur since the prisoners were already considered hopeless and helpless creatures undeserving of any kindness. To be in a prison made a person long for death. When Paul wrote to the Philippians, it was from a pit of gloom. And what did he speak about? Joy.

The word *joy* or its derivative appears fifteen times in Philippians. Given Paul's dark circumstances, the words leapt off the page signaling a light in that dismal place only the redeemed could perceive. "Rejoice in the Lord always I will say it again: Rejoice!" (v. 4). It's significant that Paul expressed this as an imperative—it's something you do, not feel according to the circumstances. Christian joy is never based on what is going on around us, but what is happening in us because of the presence of the Holy Spirit. It is also not something to be pumped up like the courage needed to enter a darkened room. Joy is the natural by-product of a life aligned with the Savior. Joy is more a symptom of one's intimacy with and reliance upon God's indwelling Holy Spirit; that is, if joy is lacking, look to your relationship with God (rather than within yourself or your circumstances).

With joy comes expectations. Regardless of the outer circumstances or who may be mistreating us, Paul said to "Let your gentleness be evident to all" (v. 5). Gentleness is understood as the willing surrender of our own personal rights. In the Septuagint it is equated with our word *noble* or used to demonstrate kindly restraint. Why do this? "The Lord is near" (v. 5). This was likely a common expression in the early church that not only voiced the hope of the Lord's return, but also was a reminder that all that now exists is only temporary. In the light of eternity, much of what was bothersome now would evaporate without a trace.

Anxiety is rejected, to be replaced instead by "prayer and petition, with thanksgiving, present[ing] your requests to God" (v. 6). Being in a constant state of anxiety is denying the power of God over our situations. Of course, there are times when we are anxious if we are in physical danger or facing an uncertain situation—that's the fight-or-flight animal instinct God gave us. Moments of anxiety in the face of threat are not the subject at hand, but rather it's the constant state of emotional anxiety that is problematic.

The antidote to the poison of anxiety is prayer and thanksgiving. When we pray we are claiming God's interest in us. Just saying a prayer is an acknowledgement of God and a realization that no matter where we are, we are never out of His sight. God is always greater than anything we face, always set on doing what is best for His child. Reminding ourselves of that reality eases any anxious feelings we might have.

Thanksgiving is part of our defense as well. Being grateful is not something restricted to a certain day in the year but like joy, a constant hallmark of the Spirit-filled believer. To be unthankful is not only wrong, but dangerous. Gordon Fee asserts that "lack of gratitude is the first step to idolatry."[1] And Karl Barth says, "Man is unguarded, open to every enemy and every danger, as long as he does not give thanks."[2]

Paul closed this section with a much beloved promise. "And the peace of God, which transcends all understanding, will guard your hearts and your minds in Christ Jesus" (v. 7). When the Bible speaks of peace, it is based on the Jewish word *shalom*, and includes the idea of a general sense of wellbeing and wholesomeness. There are times when hostilities may have ceased, but there is hardly any sense of peace in the heart.

Some families, while not in open conflict, have a pervasive seething just under the surface. Nations can stop firing at each other, but the antipathy the citizens feel toward each other hardly constitutes a desirable state. Nor can giving in to bullying behavior so as to avoid conflict be considered peace. On the other hand, there can be tremendous outer conflict and a total state of uncertainty, but a profound peace that steadies the soul. This latter idea is what Paul was speaking about. His environment was hardly peaceful, his prospects bleak at best, but he was a man dwelling in the peace that Christ gives.

Using a military metaphor, Paul said peace stood sentry as a guard over our hearts and minds. There is a paradox here in using the military framework because the military guarantees the peace with weapons of war. Paul may have been emphasizing that the peace of God was as militant in guarding our hearts, fighting against those enemies that would steal our sense of God's protection and care. This is not some pale, "peace at any price," spineless state of affairs. It is a robust, active securing of peace over and against all that is happening around.

It "transcends all understanding" (v. 7). It is a peace that, to those who are not believers, makes no sense whatsoever. Sometimes it makes no sense to us, but during times we thought we might fall apart, strength we cannot explain apart from the Lord's presence, is experienced. It goes beyond our understanding because it is, in fact, beyond us.

REFLECTION QUESTIONS

1. How would Paul express joy to others around while he was in prison?

2. In what circumstances has God guarded your heart with His peace?

28

PHILIPPIANS 4:8–9

The whole idea of a cookbook is to present not only different ideas for foods, but details on the ingredients needed, the measurements for each, steps needed for preparation, how to tell if the item is ready, and how many servings can be expected. Supposedly, whether you're an expert or a novice, following the recipe will result in your final production looking just like the picture. That is the theory, at any rate.

Having spoken about the peace of God guarding our hearts (v. 7), Paul provided the ingredients that when integrated into our thought life and practiced would result in God's peace—in His humility that transcended all the disunity and contention that wanted to dominate our lives. Like a recipe, each built on the other, and though worthwhile in and of themselves, were meant to be blended into our lives.

We are to think about what is:

True: Besides the obvious meaning of something that is not false, the word carries the idea or truthfulness and dependability. It can mean what is authentic, real, and reliable.

Noble: When we see this word we think about chivalry, and that is certainly true to what it meant in Paul's day as well. But more commonly, it referred to a moral quality that was honorable and worthy of respect.

Right: The definition of *right* was not left to individual interpretation. There was no concept of situation ethics or doing whatever felt right, varying as it did from one person to another. Rather, it meant what was right by God's standards. It included applying principles of justice.

Pure: There were two complementary ways that *pure* was applied. First, it meant to be upright and honest at a heart level that showed itself in a person's authentic attitudes, motives, and actions. It also included the idea of sexual purity for the same reasons: upright and honest with respect to the marriage bed, by abstinence when not married, and when married, fidelity to one's spouse.

Lovely: This is the only occasion that this word appears in the New Testament. It embraces not only what is beautiful but what is lovable as well. It approves of what is morally lovely and aesthetically pleasing. It would be evident in approving the good actions of a child as well as admiring a sunset.

Admirable: Dr. Gordon Fee explains, "Rather than referring to a virtue in the moral sense, it represents the kind of conduct that is worth considering because it is well spoken of by people in general."[1] It is attractive and engaging, not only to those within the church, but to people in general.

Excellent: This word was the principal term used for what was virtuous or morally excellent. To the Greek philosophers, it was essential in any discussion of ethics. It represented the highest standard people should seek to incorporate into their lives.

Praiseworthy: Any other good thing that would make for a better person is included in this catch-all word.

Paul urged the believers to "think about such things" (v. 8). There was a very strong implication that the sources of at least some of these needed not reside solely within Christianity. A beautiful piece of music, for example, is so because of the intrinsic structure and harmony, and the truth it communicates, appreciated whether the composer was a believer or not. A secular movie may have a valuable lesson that is worth considering in spite of the lifestyles of the actors, the motivation of the writers and producers, or the less-than-perfect portrayals of the characters.

This is not a call to be prudish or cloistered, turning our nose up or covering our eyes and ears at any and everything that does not have a purely religious meaning or origin. Paul urged people to sift through the elements of the culture where they lived to weigh them, knowing full well that some may be salvaged while some may have to be rejected. Someone has said, "All truth is God's truth." It can also be said that all beauty is God's beauty. Christ affirmed what the Scriptures teach us the greatest truth—the standard upon which all other laws hinge: love for God and love for neighbors. So as we think on what claims to be truth and beauty, perhaps the first measure should always be against love—as Paul described it throughout this book, love applied in terms of selfless, sacrificial humility.

Paul again referred to himself as the example (v. 9). By doing so, he reminded the Philippians that he was able to sort through what was usable in the culture and what was not. He employed discretion in the writing of this letter when he freely used military and athletic imagery, clearly secular aspects of the culture that were not influenced by the Christian message.

Further to this point, it means that when we present something to the world, whether the audience is composed of believers or not, it should be the best it can be. Thinking something will be effective simply because it is Christian is unrealistic and unbiblical. If we produce books, they should be well written. If we preach, the sermons need to be well considered and practical. If we produce magazines, movies, or design and construct buildings, they should have an attractiveness that invites people in. Even as we can glean things from the larger culture, those who are not believers should feel they can find something beautiful in the way we express our message. They must first be attracted by the loveliness of a song before being taken by what the song says.

REFLECTION QUESTIONS

1. How does Paul's list show itself in your life?

2. Do you agree with what the author has said regarding how we present the Christian message to the world? Why or why not?

29

PHILIPPIANS 4:10–13

Radio personality Steve Brown told the story of a king who was discontented. He was so anxious he couldn't sleep, think, or rest. He called his wise men and asked them what he could do. One old wise man said, "Find a man in your kingdom who is content. Then wear his shirt for a day and night, and you will be content." That sounded like a good idea, so the king ordered some of his servants to search for such a person. Days blended into weeks before his servants returned. "Where is his shirt?" asked the king. "Your majesty, he did not have one."[1]

As is for most of us today, it was uncomfortable in Paul's day to speak of one's personal financial situation, especially when things were not going well. But when the Philippians shared sacrificially with him, he opened his heart and shared a lesson with them as well. Concerning the gift they sent, he said, "I rejoice[d] greatly in the Lord that at last you renewed your concern for me" (v. 10). This is again an agricultural term: what the NIV translates *renewed* was the word used for the seasonal blossoming of a plant, much as trees that have lost their leaves bloom in the spring.

Paul wanted them to know he did not speak from his need. He told them, "I have learned to be content whatever the circumstances" (v. 11). Note that he spoke of having learned to be content. It is not natural to be content, but something acquired. Even as infants, we come forth grabbing and wanting because our survival depends on it. However, over time the grabbing and wanting goes from survival needs to all aspects of life. To learn contentment requires experience, and Paul's experience had taught him this valuable lesson.

He said he has learned to be content in need and plenty. His early Jewish upbringing and the all-embracing knowledge that came later with his conversion to Christ taught him the full meaning of David's statement: "My flesh and my heart may fail, but God is the strength of my heart and my portion forever" (Ps. 73:26). It may be true that Paul experienced his possessions being swept away as in a flood, friends treating him as a leper, and a nagging malady that felt like a thorn in his flesh; but the Lord was his portion.

On at least one occasion Paul had awakened under a pile of stones thrown in anger by his enemies. Another time he was alone, all alone, in a tiny cell with bars blocking the windows. Yet the Lord remained his portion. As sure as the Israelites found their daily ration of manna, Paul knew that for this day the Lord would be the portion he needed. And so one old man's voice lifted in song over the complaints and curses of the prison where he was. Even a prison was a cathedral in the presence of Christ.

It is most interesting that Paul went to both extremes in describing his contentment: "Whether well fed or hungry, whether living in plenty or in want" (v. 12). Ironically it can sometimes be the more difficult duty to find contentment when we have abundance. When everything is stripped away, when all that is in hand is a moldy piece of bread, it is not hard to look away to fix our eyes on Christ. But when the banquet table is full, the guest of honor can be forgotten as we gorge ourselves on the food in front of us.

In a land of plenty, the challenge to the Christian is how to handle abundance. When surrounded by gems, is it not in our nature to want to put some in our pockets? When I have a comfortable chair to sit in, is it not normal to hate the idea of getting out of it? When my stereo system reproduces the full sound of the symphony, shouldn't I want to hear it? God put us in a world of sensations, and because of that certain things will appeal to our senses. But knowing how to properly handle them takes heavenly knowledge. Paul discovered he had to know how to handle having plenty. He learned not to feast his eyes on the things in front of him, but to fix his eyes on the Lord, his Portion.

How could he do this?

"I can do all this through him who gives me strength" (v. 13).

Paul spoke this famous line in relation to the extremes of being in want and having plenty. Wherever he was on the economic ladder, whether he was in prison or walking free, no matter if his preaching brought a revival or a riot, Paul knew confidently that in these situations he was there because of God's leading. Unfortunately, in our age this verse is grossly misused to support the notion that God will help an individual to do anything from lifting weights to losing weight. While these and many other things are good ends in themselves, the verse is not to be taken as a *carte blanche* promise to be applied anywhere and everywhere apart from the condition of a person's heart and obedience to God. Paul could claim Christ's strength because he had yielded utterly to Christ's lordship.

If we are thrown in a situation too large for us, but it is by God's bidding, we can claim the verse in godly humility. If we are serving Him and are led into the valley of the shadow of death, we can selflessly claim the verse. If we find in following the Lord we are abandoned, abused, and scorned, we can love our enemies and promote their well-being by claiming this the verse. When we are in those or any other situations at the Lord's leading, what a great verse to call out with confidence! You can do everything that Christ did in sacrificing Himself for love of the world, through Him who gives you strength. Hallelujah!

REFLECTION QUESTIONS

1. Why can it seem easier to trust the Lord when we have less than when we have more?

2. What does Philippians 4:13 say to you about following where the Lord leads?

30

PHILIPPIANS 4:14–23

Henry Ford, famed founder of Ford Motor Company, was approached for a donation to build a new hospital. He pledged five thousand dollars, but was shocked to read the newspaper the next day that announced, "Henry Ford contributes fifty thousand dollars to local hospital." The fundraiser promised to have the newspaper print a retraction that read, "Henry Ford reduces his donation by forty-five thousand dollars." Knowing the reaction that this would create, Ford reluctantly agreed to raise his donation to fifty thousand dollars with one condition: over the entrance door a loose paraphrase of a biblical reference would be carved: "I came among you and you took me in" (probably Matt. 25:35).

There was none of this kind of reluctant giving among the Philippians. The culture of the day included certain understandings about how friendships were to work. As friends supporting Paul, the Philippians also shared in the humiliation and disgrace of his imprisonment.

Friendship also included the sharing of benefits. Accordingly, the gift received by Paul was consistent with this understanding. It was expected that when a specific benefit was received, something of equal value from the recipient should be given back of equal value. Quite obviously, Paul's situation made it impossible for him to reciprocate as etiquette demanded. What heightened this even more was that in giving, the Philippians' generosity was so great they put their own financial standing at risk. The Philippians understood Paul's situation and so were more than willing to waive any expectation. But it still left things feeling unfinished and out of balance.

While he was grateful for their remembrance, Paul stated again that he was not expecting any financial gift at all. But since they had given, he reported, "what I desire is that more be credited to your account" (v. 17). He noted that he appreciated not only the monetary value of what was shared, but also the thoughtfulness, calling the gifts "a fragrant offering, an acceptable sacrifice, pleasing to God" (v. 18). By hearkening back to the sacrificial system of the Old Testament, Paul reminded them there were specific requirements for the sacrifice. Among other things, the sacrificial animal had to be without blemish, not one that was sick or lame, but given at the height of its strength. It was to be only the best to make it acceptable. These friends had offered something that, had it been a temple sacrifice, would have created a beautiful fragrance whose aroma symbolically wafted upward to the throne of God.

With this, Paul rewrote the rules of the culture of the day. The gift was more than something given to him; it was an offering to God. There were now three parties involved in the transaction: God, Paul, and the Philippians. Paul could not repay them, but God could. "My God will meet all your needs according to the riches of his glory in Christ Jesus" (v. 19).

Once overwhelmed by their gift, Paul now had the Philippians overwhelmed by God's reward for their faithful giving. He called upon God to meet all their needs, careful not to imply they would have all their wants. Flemming wrote,

> The place of this promise at the climax of the letter points to a more sweeping reference. God is sufficient for *all* their needs: contentment in the face of adversity; steadfastness in the midst of opposition and suffering; divine joy and peace as an answer to anxiety; purity in a crooked world, just to name a few.[1]

God would do this "according to the riches of his glory in Christ Jesus" (v. 19). There would be no shortage, no time limit, no coming too often.

Billy Graham used to tell the story of a man walking along the road carrying a huge bundle on his back. A neighbor came alongside him in a wagon and offered him a ride home. The man gratefully accepted, but when the driver looked over, he saw the man still had the bundle on his back. "Why don't you put that down?" he asked. "No, no. I don't want to add to your burden." In the same way, our legitimate needs are in no danger of adding to God's burdens or His ability to deliver what is needed.

Paul ended his letter with his usual closing salutations. Intriguing is the reference to "those who belong to Caesar's household" (v. 22). The caesar was Nero, who was the first of the Roman emperors to persecute Christians. Yet here under that enemy there were believers, known believers, in his household. While some were no doubt slaves, church history testifies that believers were from all classes, some even blood relatives of the emperor himself.

The Christian presence was not a fluke. Their numbers continued to grow, their boldness stunning their enemies. The strange strategy initiated by the crucifixion and sealed by the resurrection was already at work. It was only a matter of time.

REFLECTION QUESTIONS

1. When have you had the opportunity to give sacrificially? How did you respond?

2. If God is willing to meet all of our needs according to His riches in Christ Jesus, what does that say about the things you want now?

NOTES

DEVOTION 1

1. David Roper, "Wonderfully Made," *Our Daily Bread*, January 2009, http://odb.org/2009/01/18/wonderfully-made/.

2. William Barclay, *The Letters of James and Peter* (Philadelphia, PA: The Westminster Press, 1960), 250.

3. James Montgomery Boice, *Philippians: An Expositional Commentary* (Grand Rapids, MI: Baker Books, 2000), 24.

DEVOTION 2

1. *The Song Book of The Salvation Army* (Alexandria, VA: The Salvation Army National Headquarters, 2016), 238.

2. Dean Flemming, *Philippians: A Commentary in the Wesleyan Tradition* (Kansas City, MO: Beacon Hill Press, 2009), 52.

DEVOTION 4

1. James Montgomery Boice, *Philippians: An Expositional Commentary* (Grand Rapids, MI: Baker Books, 2000), 47.

DEVOTION 5

1. Richard R. Melick, *The New American Commentary: Philippians, Colossians, Philemon* (Nashville, TN: Broadman Press, 1991), 73.

2. Ben Witherington, III, *Friendship and Finances in Philippi* (Valley Forge, PA: Trinity Press International, 1994), 46.

DEVOTION 7

1. Karl Barth, *Epistle to the Philippians* (Louisville, KY: Westminster John Knox Press, 2002), 55.

2. Richard R. Melick, *The New American Commentary: Philippians, Colossians, Philemon* (Nashville, TN: Broadman Press, 1991), 100.

DEVOTION 12

1. Dean Flemming, *Philippians: A Commentary in the Wesleyan Tradition* (Kansas City, MO: Beacon Hill Press, 2009), 140.

DEVOTION 15

1. Ben Witherington, III, *Friendship and Finances in Philippi* (Valley Forge, PA: Trinity Press International, 1994), 81.

2. Charles R. Swindoll, *Laugh Again* (Nashville, TN: Thomas Nelson Publishers, 1992), 104.

DEVOTION 16

1. Gordon D. Fee, *The IVP New Testament Commentary Series: Philippians* (Downer's Grove, IL: InterVarsity Press, 1999), 133.

DEVOTION 17

1. Richard DeHaan, *Daily Bread*, June 2, 1992, http://www.sermon illustrations.com/a-z/w/works_righteousness.htm.

DEVOTION 18

1. J. B. Lightfoot, *Philippians* (Wheaton, IL: Crossway Books, 1994), 163.

DEVOTION 19

1. Olivia Fecteau, "Ruling: Oceanfront home must be moved," *Turn to 10, NBC 10 WJAR, Providence, RI*, June 16, 2014, turnto10.com/ archive/ruling-ocean-front-home-must-be-moved.

2. Lorrie Cline (attributed), "I Met the Master Face to Face," quoted in Charles Swindoll, *Laugh Again* (Nashville, TN: Thomas Nelson Publishers, 1992), 122.

DEVOTION 21

1. Art Lindsley, "A Book Review, from Knowing and Doing (Winter 2002)," *C. S. Lewis Institute*, a review of David Downing, *The Most Reluctant Convert: C. S. Lewis's Journey to Faith* (Downers Grove, IL: InterVarsity Press, 2002), Dec. 30, 2016, cslewisinstitute.org/ node/48.

2. Ibid.

3. Quoted in *Ancient Christian Commentary on Scripture: Galatians, Ephesians, Philippians* (InterVarsity Press, Downers Grove, IL), 260.

DEVOTION 22

1. Charles R. Swindoll, *Laugh Again* (Nashville, TN: Thomas Nelson Publishers, 1992), 132.

2. Dean Flemming, *Philippians: A Commentary in the Wesleyan Tradition* (Kansas City, MO: Beacon Hill Press, 2009), 186.

DEVOTION 23

1. Dean Flemming, *Philippians: A Commentary in the Wesleyan Tradition* (Kansas City, MO: Beacon Hill Press, 2009), 193.

DEVOTION 24

1. C. S. Lewis, *Preface to the Screwtape Letters*, (London: Bles, 1961), x-xi.

2. John A. Knight, *Beacon Bible Commentary: Galatians through Philemon* (Kansas City: 1965), 344.

3. *Ancient Christian Commentary on Scripture: Galatians, Ephesians, Philippians* (Downer's Grove, IL: 1999), 263.

DEVOTION 25

1. Ben Witherington, III, *Friendship and Finances in Philippi* (Valley Forge, PA: Trinity Press International, 1994), 98.

2. John A. Knight, *Beacon Bible Commentary: Galatians through Philemon* (Kansas City: 1965), 345.

DEVOTION 26

1. Richard R. Melick, Jr. *The New American Commentary: Philippians, Colossians, Philemon* (Nashville, TN: Broadman Press, 1991), 146.

2. *Ancient Christian Commentary on Scripture* (Downers Grove, IL: 1999), 214.

3. Allen Satterlee. *Notable Quotables: A Compendium of Gems from Salvation Army Literature* (Atlanta: 1985), 241.

DEVOTION 27

1. Gordon D. Fee, *The IVP New Testament Commentary Series: Philippians* (Downer's Grove, IL: InterVarsity Press, 1999), 175.

2. Karl Barth, *Epistle to the Philippians* (Louisville, KY: Westminster John Knox Press, 2002), 123.

DEVOTION 28

1. Gordon D. Fee, *The IVP New Testament Commentary Series: Philippians* (Downer's Grove, IL: InterVarsity Press, 1999), 113.

DEVOTION 29

1. James Condon, "The Power of Attitude," *Pipeline*, February, 2013.

DEVOTION 30

1. Dean Flemming, *Philippians: A Commentary in the Wesleyan Tradition* (Kansas City, MO: Beacon Hill Press, 2009), 247.

The COLLECTOR'S Eye

Decorating with the Objects You Love

CHRISTINE CHURCHILL

with Ted Loos

PHOTOGRAPHS BY

Keith Scott Morton

HarperResource

An Imprint of HarperCollinsPublishers

FIRST EDITION

DESIGNED BY SUSI OBERHELMAN

Printed on acid-free paper

Library of Congress Cataloging-In-Publication Data
Churchill, Christine.
    The collector's eye : decorating with the objects you love / by Christine
Churchill.
        p. cm.
    Includes index
    ISBN 0-688-17386-1 (alk. paper)
        1. Collectibles—United States. 2. Antiques—United States.
    3. Collectors and collecting—United States. I. Title.
    NK1125.C47 2002
    747—dc21   2001026382

02 03 04 05 06 TP 10 9 8 7 6 5 4 3 2 1

WITH LOVE AND GRATITUDE TO MY FATHER,
JAMES F. CHURCHILL,
WHOSE CODE OF SIMPLE ELEGANCE
WILL ALWAYS BE REMEMBERED

Contents

SLEUTHING for Style

IT ISN'T EXACTLY A NEWS FLASH: beautiful surroundings make for a better life. When it comes to figuring out how to make those surroundings beautiful, well, that's the tricky part, and hence the genesis of this book. For starters, take a look into the homes of the seasoned collectors that follow, and immerse yourself in rooms that feature the objects they love. The stylish interiors you're about to see have a decidedly personal twist, and getting those great looks didn't require a decorator.

To some, the very idea of collecting "smalls" still smacks of Victorian vitrines crammed with porcelain do-dads. In the modern visions featured here, it's a satisfying process that requires a bit of knowledge and, sometimes, a bit of restraint. And these smart folks have learned how to rely on their own quirky good taste. Whether it's working with a trusted dealer or browsing a favorite auction website, there are lots of ways to get in on the treasure hunt. Some might even stop by a couple of local shops on the way home from the supermarket. That's how Gretchen Mann acquired many of her shapely architectural finials, featured in "Drawn to Scale."

Sleuthing for style, as I call it, is a process that begins with an appetite for shopping the vintage market, and it doesn't hurt to love the thrill of the chase. When I was fifteen, I bought my first vintage item—a perfect pale green suede dress from the 1940s. I didn't realize at the time that this purchase was the first hint of a collector's mentality that would end up shaping my life. Meaning, I don't just buy shoes, I collect them; and when I travel, finding flea markets and little shops in every town is my way of delving into a bit of social history. But if looking for fine objects sounds intellectual, it gets visceral sooner than you can say "hotel silver." When your heart starts beating fast in fear that you've missed out, you know you're hooked.

This book features nearly forty different collectibles, the majority of which are considered to be more vintage than antique. It celebrates the inherent value and timeless quality of good design, that, not coincidentally,

▶ THE ORDER OF THINGS: **a miscellany of midcentury glass vases (opposite), ranging in price from $8 to $100 all get star treatment and plenty of breathing space aloft silver-leaf cubes. Choosing pieces that are about the same size heightens the impact of the grid pattern.**

9

▶ BOLDLY REPEATED SHAPES **of spheres and pillars (above) are seen in both objects and furniture. Decorating out of the box: Hoffman's geometric prints add a clever twist when juxtaposed with a traditional wing chair covered in crewel fabric (opposite).**

invites constant reinterpretation. Some objects, like wireware salad washers, seem too prosaic to relate to today's sleek, pared-down look. But when you consider their clean lines—not to mention their function-ality—suddenly they seem modern indeed.

For the collectors who appreciate them, it's all about good forms and interesing shapes. Objects are used as focal points, often in place of art, simply because there is no better way to make a statement. All you have to do is look at Jason and Robyn Rubinstein's home in "Presented in Technicolor" to see this idea in action. And if you think it's getting tougher to find great pieces, you're right. These collectors will share trade secrets on how and where they came by their collections, and will have a few bargain tips, too. Through their stories, you'll learn how today's most interest-ing rooms got that way.

Whether it's updated country, the com-fort of Arts and Crafts, or midcentury modern,

THE COLLECTOR'S EYE

collections drive the decorating scheme. The objects are emblematic of your look and inspire all the other design details. Savvy organization of them maximizes their impact. You can create a stunning tableau with dozens of the same type, as George Waffle does with his Burley Winter pottery in "True to Textures," or distill a big idea with a few choice gems. It used to be that five of anything made a collection: well, I think three would do. In any case, these treasures are meant to be used, displayed, touched, and lived with.

The old definitions of collector and dealer are disappearing. Today, the best dealers are selling more than just objects. They're purveyors of an aesthetic brand all their own, and are often masters at the art of display. It takes a confident eye to see the potential in old gas station signs as did Pamela Fritz in "Elements of Alchemy," but that's when the real fun begins.

Perhaps the most important lesson learned from these collectors is Trading Up and Paring Down. It's a mindset I'm personally familiar with: as you'll see in the upcoming pages, I live in a New York apartment, where space constraints can be a challenge. But limitations can often be turned into virtues. The more specific you become about what you collect, the better the results. Along the way, you have to fine-tune your collecting, letting go of some objects in order to acquire others. Paring

A FRIEZE OF **cobalt blue bottles (opposite), some of which cost less than a dollar, frame the view in antiques dealer/ collector Judy Naftulin's country cottage. Above: The Great Wall of China, as she calls it, is Judy's graphic protest against mimimalism. Just as long as they are blue and white, transferware plates go up as they're found, and range in both quality and condition.**

down yields new insights, and makes way for better choices based on experience. If you abide by an evolutionary process, your home will reflect the ultimate reward: comfort and personality, all your own.

So don't wait—start collecting!

13

Certain places have a glow we associate with a particular season, like Paris in April or Venice in late August. When the first decent light of spring—still a bit pale and shining in low from the south—penetrates this western Connecticut retreat, it breathes fresh air into a home

LAKE Effects

that has usually weathered a gloomy, gray winter. Collector Scott Weaver, a New York–based architect, comes here to escape the rigors of city life. The large, shingle-style camp house was built in the 1890s, and it houses his meticulously chosen collection of mercury glass and Arts and Crafts pottery and furniture.

Weaver revels in all the details that define his profession. He also does interior design, so for him, working with the available natural light, in springtime or any other season, is standard procedure. He also has a built-in light enhancer—a shimmering lake just outside his front door that throws rays over several remarkable collections.

Born and raised in Ohio, Weaver came to his aesthetic sense at the heels of his grandfather, a dealer-picker-inventor whose carriage-house workshop was filled to the rafters with bits and pieces of the past. Having love of family tied to love of design at such an early age helps explain Weaver's reverence toward beautiful objects. He had his priorities straight from the start—one of Weaver's first commissions was paid for in part with the client's underappreciated Arts and Crafts bookcase.

Weaver moved to New York in the early 1990s to work on architectural projects with the firms of Peter Marino and the late Jed Johnson. "Moving to New York was a real eye-opener," Weaver says. "I was exposed to the absolute best—right down to the smallest piece of hardware."

Since starting his own company, his work with clients now includes shopping for furnishings and antiques. Weaver thinks of collecting as a basic system of work and rewards: If you put in enough time and energy, there's no limit to what you can achieve. The "right"

GENTLE MORNING LIGHT **in a guest bedroom (opposite) highlights the contrast between the rough-hewn white birch bark wall panels and the shiny silver of mercury glass vases and platters. The black outline of the English Arts and Crafts spindle chairs and table adds a dark panache to this otherwise monochromatic scheme. Above: A mid-nineteenth-century mercury glass vase is etched with tropical tree and bush forms; it sits atop a display bracket fashioned from a birch branch.**

MERCURY Glass

Many collectors believe mercury glass was first made as an inexpensive sterling silver substitute, but it soon developed into its own separate art form. First produced in the late eighteenth century, mercury glass is hand-blown, double-walled glass with an interior coating of silver-colored metal compounds. It was used in a wide range of forms (opposite), including candlestick holders, compotes, candy dishes, plates, goblets, wig stands, curtain tiebacks, and other articles.

It reached its broadest popularity in the mid to late nineteenth century. Back then, high-quality European- and American-made pieces were lightweight, had graceful forms, and were decorated with acid-etched fruit or floral motifs, wheel-turned cut glass designs, and sometimes paint. The details were intended as equals to the finest decoration on other forms of glass and china. The popularity and quality of mercury glass waned in the twentieth century, but it has always remained in production.

▶ MERCURY GLASS PIECES **are growing harder
to find. Among Weaver's rarities are two-piece covered dishes
(above left) and a European compote detailed with a gold-washed
interior (above right). Opposite: Three chock-full shelves of the
collection display the wide range of forms found in mercury glass,
including delicate pairs of etched vases from the early 1800s; late-
nineteenth-century American coffee mugs; and spiky faux candles
from the 1950s kept in the vase on the bottom shelf. Weaver hired
chemists to prematurely oxidize the new unfinished wood cabinets to give them the patina of century-old wood.**

piece — in terms of age, condition, and look —
is out there somewhere, just waiting.

For a man whose personal tastes run
to the carefully hand-hewn finishes associated with Arts and Crafts objects, mercury
glass might seem an unusually glitzy choice.

He now has over 200 pieces of this beguiling
glass, and he's bought them wherever he
could find a prime example — markets, dealers, and auctions.

His favorite pieces are a pair of vases
with unusual swag details that live in his
kitchen cabinets. They set him back $1,500,
but Weaver says he couldn't resist the "unique
pieces that are also so impressive, and in pristine condition." Most of his glass was far
cheaper, often under $500 for each object.

In the guest bedroom, Weaver pan-
eled the room with birch tree bark and
designed a display for the glass right on the

▶ WILLIAM MORRIS **wallpaper surrounds an English Arts and Crafts chair and an American wicker writing table in one of Weaver's guest rooms (above). It's a bookish grouping that makes for an ideal study area. Opposite: The top of the writing table holds a small, choice collection of Sicard vases made by Weller Pottery of Zanesville, Ohio. They are accompanied by the blotter, calendar, and inkwell from a bronze-and-glass, Pine Cone–pattern desk set by Louis Comfort Tiffany. All the furniture and objects have British and American origins dating from 1880 and 1920.**

wall. Juxtaposing the silvery forms against the white bark creates a swirl of bright, complementary textures. "Sunlight is rare in that room, and I knew that that would lighten it up," says Weaver. "Most of what comes into the room is reflected off the lake."

Getting the full indoor effect of a natural outdoor mirror took a heroic effort, but Weaver's not the type to take shortcuts. First, he had to find the bark, which in this case came

from a forester who knows how to harvest it without killing the tree. The bark arrived in random sizes up to four feet square, pressed flat between planks of plywood, and was cut to a uniform grid of two feet square. Then it was glued neatly to the wall. Once installed, the seams between the bark panels were covered with birch branches split lengthwise, like a log. All this handling had to be completed without harming the bark's delicate surface.

Birch wasn't a random choice. "It's an indigenous tree around here," says Weaver, "and there are some antique birch sconces in the living room that were original to the house." That sense of an Adirondack retreat might seem at odds with his William Morris wallpaper—more likely to conjure up a Lake District country home in England—but all these elements harmonize beautifully. Weaver, like all talented designers, knows the value of playing against type. The glass is the most unexpected object of all here by the lake, but it's also the one that most clearly beckons: Dive in.

▶ **THE MASTER BEDROOM holds a large suite of English faux bamboo furniture from the 1880s (opposite). Weaver has combined it with a gray-green leather easy chair, stenciled and embroidered Arts and Crafts curtain panels, and metal-clad pottery by Clewell. The delicate wicker table lamp was a very popular early electric lighting form in American Arts and Crafts homes; they carry a price premium if found in perfect condition today.**

CLEWELL Pottery

Clewell pottery was made during the studio art pottery movement that coincided with the American Arts and Crafts period. Its maker, Charles W. Clewell of Canton, Ohio, would clad earthenware forms purchased from local potteries with a thin layer of copper, bronze, or silver for the sole purpose of manipulating the metals' natural oxidation process. His original art form spotlighted the beauty of the metal itself—not the earthenware or the glazes, as was the case with other producers. Clewell's secret techniques allowed him to produce an amazing range of seemingly natural (yet man-made) hues of tarnished blues, greens, and ambers. Clewell produced his wares from 1906 until his death in 1965.

No matter how good their instincts, all collectors rely

on serendipity. When Jason and Robyn Rubinstein

walked into New York's Pier Show ten years ago, they

had no idea what was in store for them. "To our right-

PRESENTED
in Technicolor

hand side was this mesmerizing, beautifully colored

glass," says Jason. "I'll never forget the scene." What

he stumbled upon was a display of Blenko glass, from

one of America's only homegrown, handcrafted glass

companies. It was all large, striking, and—best of all—

cheap. "We looked at each other and said, 'This is

ridiculous,'" recalls Jason. "Let's take it all." So they picked up twenty amazing vases and jugs from one of Blenko's best periods, the suddenly experimental 1950s and 1960s.

"Fortunately, what we paid for 80 percent of our collection is what each piece costs now," says Robyn. Though Blenko glass is hardly expensive these days—it's still rare to find a piece for over $100—there are very few opportunities to create a stunning, multi-piece tableau in one fell swoop.

The Rubinsteins have installed their candy-colored collection, appropriately enough, in the upper two floors of a Greenwich Village town house with a colorful history. The house, built in 1850, is a former speakeasy. "If these walls could talk, they would speak of sin," jokes Jason.

Though they haven't tried to whitewash their house's past, they did choose to paint the bricks white, providing a suitable blank canvas for their brightly hued objects and eclectic furniture. Working with their longtime decorator, Morrie Breyer, the Rubinsteins have blended Blenko with their other areas of interest, especially outsider and tramp art.

One thing is clear: Jason and Robyn like their art bold and idiosyncratic. Blenko is just the beginning. A gorgeous pastel by famed outsider artist Thornton Dial, for instance, hangs next to an elaborate Adirondack-style sideboard made partially with bark-on birch tree limbs.

THE RUBINSTEINS' RENOVATED **galley kitchen (left) is a perfect setting for a roundup of Blenko housewares, including some gigantic tumblers with a double-ring design. The mosaic flowerpot, one of many creations by six-year-old daughter Jesse, sparkles with primary colors. Above: A wooden bowl makes the perfect repository for fishbobs, the colored glass balls used by fishermen in their nets. Pressed into service for a new purpose, they make great replacements for any missing decanter tops.**

29

A few small works on paper have the distinctly free-handed look of the other outsider pieces, but they turn out to be by six-year-old Jesse Rubinstein. Their daughter is not only a budding artist, she's also a collector herself. "We asked her to pick out one thing she wanted to collect," says Robyn. "She picked out these clear medicine bottles, but her limit is seven dollars."

It's no wonder Jesse took so quickly to the collecting bug: The atmosphere chez Rubinstein encourages creativity in all its forms. "As consultants for the last few years, we spend a tremendous amount of time at home," says Jason of their focus on perfecting every square foot of the three thousand they own. "We work here, and every dollar we make goes back into our home."

Blenko glass in particular is a lot more stimulating for a workspace than your average fabric-covered cubicle wall. Most of it is situated on either side of the town house's old fireplace, toward the far southern end of their dining room, so it gets frequent, strong sunlight. "It's happy," says Robyn. "Every-

EVEN THOUGH THE DINING AREA **contains lots of objects, intentionally spare furnishings make for an airy balance. With a bright white backdrop, custom-built shelves make for a striking display of 1950s- and 1960s-era Blenko glass. The variety of colors and sizes also shows a good range of relative value. With Blenko, size commands attention and higher prices. Intense colors like Ruby, Persian, Amethyst, and Jonquil are favored, and Turquoise (known to collectors as Blenko Blue) and Tangerine are both popular and prevalent.**

BLENKO Glass

The eighty-year history of Blenko Handcraft is a lesson in timing—good, bad, and totally unpredictable. William John Blenko, a hard-headed Englishman, tried three times to found a handcrafted glass business in the United States. He finally made it work on his fourth try, in 1921, settling in Milton, West Virginia. He was sixty-seven.

Blenko first called his company the Eureka Art Glass Co. because he had spent years trying to perfect ruby-red-colored sheet glass, one of the hardest shades to pull off technically. Once he got it right, he was doing a good business selling his mouth-blown sheet glass to churches. His product went into the restoration of the great Reims Cathedral, among others.

Strangely, the company took off when many other enterprises were failing. In 1929, a distributor asked Blenko to make some tableware, and a whole new product line was born. Then in the 1930s, Colonial Williamsburg awarded Blenko the contract to reproduce the eighteenth-century glassware for its historic site.

Blenko has always been known for its intensely bright colors. In the 1950s and 1960s, three successive designers—Winslow Anderson, Wayne Husted, and Joel Myers—were encouraged to experiment with shapes, and they produced some of the wonderfully eccentric glassware of the era. Even bad timing proved useful: Blenko's famous bent-necked decanter came about when one of the blowers left the glass cylinder in the furnace too long.

Now run by the founder's great-grandson, Richard Blenko, the company is enjoying a new wave of popularity due to unprecedented interest in collecting the vintage examples.

thing we collect has that in common. It makes you smile."

But that childlike criterion belies the sophistication in every choice. The mid-century Blenko works they favor all share a certain funky profile—just about to get silly, but still this side of elegant. "It's very modern," says Jason. "We felt we could live with this glass."

They have also cleverly combined the Blenko with round glass balls called "fish-bobs," used by some fishermen on their lines; they stand in for the original stoppers missing from some of the Blenko decanters. They're almost too casual an item to call a collection, but they cap a smart look for around $15 a piece. (They actually bought a whole bowlful for $25.) "You see them strung up in tacky seafood restaurants," says Robyn, "but they just look right here."

The Rubinsteins only rarely sleuth around for more Blenko, since they're spoiled by having paid so little for it ten years ago. Occasionally they'll acquire a couple of new items. Last year Robyn left a silent bid of $30 for two medium-sized pieces at a Braswell Galleries auction in Norwalk, Connecticut—and got them.

When Jason describes Blenko as "poor man's Murano," don't let him fool you. The Rubinsteins are well aware that Blenko has made their interior rich indeed.

▶ THE ZIGGURAT SHELF BRACKETS **add a retro dimension to the dining area's painted brick walls (left). Above: The kitchen's width accommodates a 1930s glass and metal bar cart, another ode to good vintage design and a practical companion to a rotating assortment of Blenko decanters.**

35

During the day, this loft apartment high above a busy

Greenwich Village street seems quiet, cool, and calm.

The home of writer Ted Jones, located on the top

floor of an 1890s manufacturing loft, has few walls.

A feeling of openness pervades the place, and the

A VIRTUOSO
Performance

bold colors encourage you to move between the

loosely designated areas. The high ceilings undulate

in a series of barrel vaults, providing a concert hall-

like framework for a top collection of midcentury

American modern furniture and accessories. At night,

the apartment and its contents ignite in a sophisticated and slightly wild way that recalls the hipster movies of the 1960s —*Blow-Up* set in New York instead of London. In headier times, the Bauhaus-era apartment was inhabited by design legend Jack Lenor Larsen, giving it yet another claim to its mod legacy.

Jones, a collector with a wide range of interests, seized the chance to transform the atelier, giving it his own brand of elegant, low-key comfort. "It's a nurturing environment," he says, "and it doesn't put on airs." That's not the usual way people talk about modern spaces, which is precisely why the hard edges of minimalism and Jetson-era clichés are nowhere to be found. Ironic as it may be, even with so many icons of modern design present and accounted for, the space manages to seem downright cozy.

Virtuoso performances are many: The floating platform sofa and Tiffany glass tiled table designed by Edward Wormley for Dunbar achieve a sort of lyric grace that perfectly fits the vision of this Manhattan collector fifty years later.

The secret to this successful symphony? The soft curves of 1950s French furniture and lighting by Jean Prouvé, Charlotte Perriand, and Jean Royère—along with the familiar substantiality of American Arts and Crafts classics—temper any tendency towards contrivance.

▶ A SUAVE DINING AREA **grouping in the large main living area comes together (opposite) with a curved 1950s Vladimir Kagan settee upholstered in coarse silk, two Alvar Aalto chairs from the Finnish Pavilion at the 1939 World's Fair, and an oval Saarinen dining table. Decorating the tabletop are three examples from the famous Pulcini glass birds series designed by Alessandro Pianon for Vistosi in 1962. Nearby, a colorful glass mobile (above) from the 1960s by Michael and Frances Higgins catches light from a frosted skylight.**

Sculptural shapes abound. The many George Nelson clocks scattered throughout are tactile gems prized for their whimsical and unique qualities. "I was attracted to all of these modern forms because they seemed to be part of the same design spirit," Jones says of his collections. That spirit undeniably reflects the exuberance of the mid-twentieth century, when easy living seemed like a birthright.

According to Jones, because the designs are still only fifty or so years old, current buyers are sometimes still able to obtain items from the original owners—and sometimes even from the designers themselves. For example, Vladimir Kagan, a leading 1950s decorator and designer, still maintains a shop in New York City. Unlike collecting Early American objects with a provenance connected to people long dead, these modern masterpieces have, in many cases, a living oral history at the ready.

"The people who originally bought modern in the 1940s and 1950s are almost

▶ IN ANOTHER CORNER **of the main room, a monumental glass screen made by Michael and Frances Higgins in the 1950s serves as a backdrop for a sleek, tufted sofa designed by Edward Wormley for Dunbar, an Eero Saarinen Womb Chair, and a pair of Saarinen side tables. The screen is an assemblage of pieces from at least four different sources nationwide, and the whimsical bird-shaped birdcage between the windows was found in a thrift store in San Francisco.**

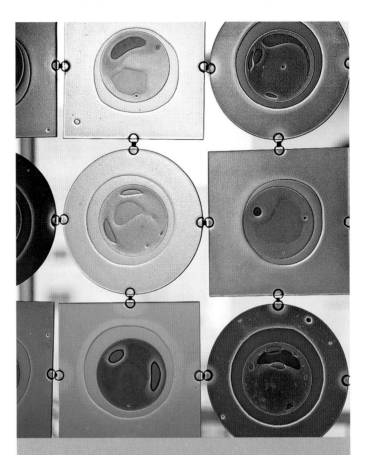

HIGGINS Glass

In the 1950s, glass artists Michael and Frances Higgins created the rondaley, a heat-laminated colored glass disk outfitted with connecting metal rings used to, make wall hangings, window screens, room dividers and mobiles. Bright, colorful, textural, and distinctly period, the disks come in round or square shapes, three sizes—6-, 9-, and 12-inch diameters—and over 200 colors. In production for decades, they are usually unmarked and are now showing up at antiques markets, often misidentified; prices range greatly from $75 to $250 a piece, depending on size. The Higgins, also produced a wide range of other glass objects, including jewelry, tableware, ashtrays, and light fixtures.

41

▶ THE BEDROOM SITTING AREA **is filled with beloved objects that didn't seem to go anywhere else. The over-stuffed George Smith sofa, the 1950s Jean Prouvé table and chair (foreground), and an inexpensive 1960s teak and enameled metal table from Norway look happy to have found one another. Various George Nelson clocks are tucked in here and there. The photo opposite highlights another Higgins glass screen, a teak chest by George Nelson, an Arts and Crafts Plail Bros. chair, and, outside the window, the building's original neoclassical column capital.**

without exception interesting people, and they're still alive," says Jones. "They were architects, academics, design professionals of some sort, and they loved buying these objects and furniture when they were young. They'll talk your ear off."

Not that he minds. Jones's passion for the material has led him to follow the best pieces wherever they may be, and he has watched the auction market closely for

THE CLOCK SERIES by George Nelson for the Howard Miller Clock Company started with very simple designs based on circles, squares, and cones, and then grew progressively wilder. The Chess Piece clocks (above left) were part of the 1957 Baroque Series. The Kaleidoscope Clock (rear, above right) and the rare Floating Mine Clock (opposite, left) both date to 1960. The two small clocks (opposite, right) are early gems from 1951. The skill of the clock company woodworkers gave the series its charm, and modern-day collectors gave most of the clocks their individual names.

many years. A few road trips to dealers in the Chicago area turned up some choice finds, and his trained eye alighted on a gem or two at antique and flea markets. All told, the collections took about four or five years to assemble, and in that period many of the items, although expensive at the time, have doubled in value.

Jones has been around the block enough to know the dos and don'ts of the trade by now. He cautions that if you're lucky, high modern furniture will have its original fabric in good condition. Most likely, it won't. So he did what any smart person does—he asked for a second opinion, calling in another designer to consult on fabrics and wall colors.

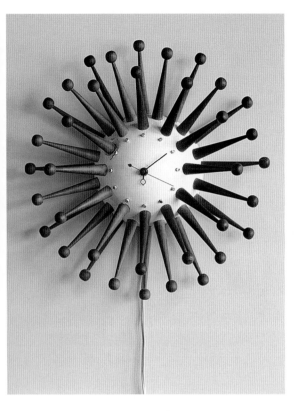

You could say that the resulting scheme blows hot and cold. The collector used his instincts when thinking color, and true to midcentury form, decided he could have it all. One end of the apartment speaks in warm woods and breathless reds, and the other talks the talk of cool blues and mauves. In the bedroom, when it came time to decide on how to frame forty-eight vintage photographs, his designer suggested using colored mattes, a detail they both remembered from the lushly brilliant set-decorating of the film *Indiscreet*.

Fortuny fabric was used to trim the waterfall of sheer curtains, and vivid stripes and checks from a box of 1950s swatches

NELSON Clocks

Between 1949 and 1963, well-known architect and magazine editor George Nelson and his New York–based design firm produced about 140 modern clock designs for the Howard Miller Clock Company of Zeeland, Michigan. The series was conceived as functional modern sculpture for the new American post–World War II home, to coordinate with Nelson's furniture designs for another family concern, the Herman Miller Furniture Company. The series includes several modern design icons, the Ball Clock (1949), the Asterisk Clock, and the Spike Clock (both 1952).

As the series evolved, the idea of a clock as a piece of sculpture often outweighed its basic time-telling function. Prices start at about $500 but can soar past $10,000 for rare models in unusual color combinations.

45

▶ THE MASTER BEDROOM **strikes a note of playful nostalgia. The owner pushed two George Nelson Thin Edge twin beds together to form a king-sized bed. The light fixture is by Jean Royère. The forty-eight framed photos capture the costumes of showgirls and specialty acts at New York's Ritz Theater in the 1920s, and were found at the 26th Street flea market in New York. The small glass mosaic-topped table is a 1950s design by Edward Wormley for Dunbar.**

bought at auction were used for pillows. When it came to reupholstering, Jones's designer went to a handful of contemporary fabric sources like Jack Lenor Larsen, Maharam, and Knoll. Luckily, all of them had revived some of their best patterns that had anchored their lines more than forty years ago.

The apartment gives lie to many of the myths about midcentury modern. It's no longer kitsch, and it's no longer a secondary

field of collecting for people waiting until they can afford more traditional antiques. The philosophy of modernism, often overlooked in favor of its easily appreciable boldness, was that function is paramount, but function with beauty is ideal. From here, it looks like prosperity with a purpose.

TODAY'S MODERN COLLECTORS avidly seek examples of the Paolo Venini–designed hourglasses, called *clessidre*, made by Venini in the 1950s and 1960s. They were made by hand blowing each colored orb separately, and then joining them together later in a process called *incalmo*. They come in three sizes, 5, 7, and 9 inches, and in a wide range of colors. Here, a small collection sits on a bright window ledge overlooking a balcony furnished with two chairs made by the Salterini Company in the 1940s.

Some say beauty is in the eye of the beholder. But

at the Brooklyn brownstone of Tom Dolle and George

Waffle, it may be in the fingertips instead. These

determined flea marketers have several different

twentieth-century collections, but their two most

TRUE to Textures

interesting passions share one trait—a texture both

sensual and unusual. When a friend introduced

Dolle to the pewter bowls and platters of little-

known Russian emigré Serge Nekrassoff, he was

hooked. "They were all hand-hammered and hand-

made," says Dolle, who runs his own graphic design

firm in New York City. "They all have a very 'hammery' finish, and we just love that naturalistic feel."

Nekrassoff was inspired by the Arts and Crafts movement, and much of his work reflects that style, though he continued to work well after its heyday. Dolle and Waffle have purchased about forty of his pieces from the 1930s and 1940s. "The room where we have the most pieces has an Arts and Crafts feel, so we thought it was appropriate there," says Dolle. They've made a deliberate effort to avoid display. The stacks of plates and platters add to an atmosphere of casual deshabille.

Though built in 1879 at the height of the Victorian era, the Dolle-Waffle abode displays many decorative arts from the first half of the twentieth century—but very few of the usual suspects. Instead, they've gone off the beaten track to more remote regions of the collecting world.

"Real Arts and Crafts metalware is better known, and more expensive," says Waffle,

▶ THIS NEKRASSOFF PLATTER **(left), probably done in the 1940s, brings a fairy-tale sensibility to the form of a leaf. The warm textures of the Burley Winter vase and the wall's leathery paint treatment create a steady visual hum. Right: When pewter was scarce during World War II, Nekrassoff also used copper for his metalwork. Although it is more rare, Dolle and Waffle have stacks of work in both materials.**

NEKRASSOFF Pewter

Russian-born Serge Nekrassoff settled in Darien, Connecticut, in 1931. He began producing pieces with his unique method of hammering metal, one that allowed him to create a forged finish without heating it to high temperatures. Working mainly in pewter, he juxtaposed its distressed surface with the delicate curves and whimsical details of leaves, vines, and flowers. In the 1950s he moved to Florida and became famous for his colorful enamel plates, which often featured stylized birds.

Don't be fooled by Nekrassoff pewter that's being passed off as the earlier (and more expensive) Arts and Crafts fare. It's almost always marked with the NEKRAS stamp (earlier pieces) or with a simple "Nekrassoff" in script (after 1930). Flea markets are perfect sources for the metalwork that looks like it was forged in fairyland.

53

a researcher who specializes in gardens. "It's all been discovered. We prefer the undiscovered." In this case, the item itself plays along. Nekrassoff pewter tends to go undercover in many markets, looking like "gray nothing" in Dolle's words, until it meets with some spit and polish. Hence, most people don't know what they have, and they bought most of their pieces for under $75. The rarest versions can now go for $800.

Neither of this ambitious pair collected much of anything before they bought the brownstone in 1990. Ever since they acquired the extra space, it's been one long treasure hunt. "We love flea marketing," says Dolle. "We're true bargain hunters." And as for ebay, they'd prefer to buy in person. "It's much better to pick up a piece and touch it," says Waffle. "Establish a relationship with it."

At one point these supremely tactile collectors had established a relationship with some 500 pieces of McCoy pottery. They sold about half of that collection, and in the process came across a more obscure Ohio pottery maker, Burley Winter. For Dolle, who hails from that state, it was a thrill to find a new name from there—and

▶ FOR THEIR DEN, the collectors have mixed a period craftsman chair, circa 1910, with reproduction cabinets by the Gustav Stickley Company. Among their many pottery pieces, the 20-inch-high jardiniere pedestal by Burley Winter is a favorite, since these more monumental shapes were all the rage in the 1920s and 1930s. The Nekrassoff pewter pitcher on top of the left cabinet is a rare example of that shape.

55

BURLEY WINTER
Pottery

The Burley Winter Pottery Company may have been one of forty or so potteries operating in the small town of Crooksville, Ohio, during the late nineteenth and early twentieth centuries, but its distinctive Arts and Crafts style and unique glazes set it apart from the rest.

Like Lazalier and Clewell, other lesser-known potteries that flourished on the rich clay of the Ohio River Valley, Burley Winter began as a producer of simple, inexpensive utilitarian tableware. Early pieces are easily identified by the unique heart-shaped mark and embossed BURLEY WINTER that potters pressed into the bottoms of bowls and vases. The tankard and mug sets that Burley Winter produced during its early years are particularly plentiful, but don't count on finding a mark; some pieces are merely numbered on the bottom.

Today, Burley Winter pottery bearing the distinctive, decorative glazes that potters developed during the company's heyday are grabbing the spotlight from their more demure predecessors. The colorful glazes often blended slightly during the firing process, resulting in one-of-a-kind pieces. Burley fans vie for the best quality glazes—and the more outlandish, the better.

Especially prized are the vases Burley Winter produced with "punchouts" in the bottom that the factory had wired for use as lamps. Rarest of all are the working lamps themselves, complete with hardware and accessories. Very few remain, and lucky is the collector who comes across one.

▶ A REFRESHING CHANGE **from the hot colors of the Burley Winter is the cool blue McCoy pottery collection in the brownstone's bedroom. Though McCoy is a much more recognized name, Dolle and Waffle have stayed true to form with their love of the unusual: The cobalt glaze is the rarest and most sought after of all McCoy colors, as it was known to infect the other glazes during production. Lamps like the one pictured opposite are especially prized.**

one that came from the same town, Roseville, as McCoy and many more famous names.

But the quirky look was what made it truly alluring. "With Burley, it's all about the glaze, and the texture of the glaze," says Dolle. The rough surfaces and strange colors of the pottery truly transform the fairly basic and classical shapes of the urns, pots, and vases. The most frequent glazes were a hot pink-gray combination and a green-terra cotta melding. Though mostly produced in the 1930s, its funky colors were a precursor to the palette specific to 1950s home design.

It's the kind of collection that needs great care in display, and many of the pieces have been placed against a wall that has been treated with a leather-textured paint. Instead of being overwhelming, these two unusual surfaces rub each other exactly the right way.

The den that holds most of the Burley Winter and Nekrassoff gives off a warm and creative glow, as if you're in an artist's studio. "We've tried to make sense of this stuff visually," says Waffle. "We always go after shapes and colors that work well together."

The organic flourishes of Nekrassoff's platters—tendrils, leaf shapes, and buds—are offset by the purely surface effects of the pottery. "The textures of the pewter and the pottery work really well together," says Dolle, "since they're both a bit crude in their way." He's right, but it takes a couple of refined minds to combine them so artfully.

It's only the very first moment that you think that Tricia Foley's house is all white. On the contrary— once your eyes adjust, you can see that her historic home on Long Island is actually a symphony of creams, pearls, and the very faintest roses. For Foley,

PLATES of the Day

a noted designer and editor, this subtly vibrant look has become her signature. "I think it's a really serene backdrop for my life, which is kind of crazy," she says. "It's very quiet and peaceful." The small week-end house—it's less than 1,000 square feet—is a "bay and a half" cape-style house from the 1840s.

Foley has owned it for twenty years, and she has filled out the footprint over time to make use of every possible space while "retaining the integrity of the house," as she puts it. She added a guest room in the unfinished attic and even dug out the dirt cellar to make a laundry room.

But her real ingenuity has gone into the design of the rooms themselves. "I think it's the color palette that ties it all together," says Foley. And the result gives lie to the idea that

▶ LOOKING FROM THE LIVING ROOM **into the kitchen of the house (left), a stack of Nantucket lightship baskets acts as a style beacon. Foley uses these reproduction baskets, which have an unusually tight weave, to store photographs and clippings—typical of the functionality she prizes. The hand-blown glass vase at right may date to the early twentieth century and was probably used for wine or olive oil. Above: Diverse eras happily mingle in Foley's living room. Among glassware, the nineteenth-century ship's decanter (the base is extra heavy so it wouldn't tip on the stormy seas) looks right at home across from the mantel's Federal-style glass lanterns, which are new.**

65

CREAMWARE

It seems like a strange marriage: 200-year-old creamware plates stacked on a $75 Ikea table. But back in the 1700s, creamware played a similar role to the one Ikea does today: it provided an inexpensive and stylish alternative.

Josiah Wedgwood's creamware replaced wood and pewter on the tables of the European and American middle classes during the second half of the eighteenth century, one of the achievements that has made his last name synonymous with quality tableware.

As much mad scientist as potter by trade, Wedgwood began experimenting with a cream-colored glazed earthenware in his Burslem, England, workshop, known as the "Ivy House" Works in 1762. Staffordshire potters had been searching for a way to imitate Chinese porcelain since 1750, but Wedgwood's version of the lightweight, buff-colored ware with a transparent glaze was undeniably the most popular. Even Queen Charlotte fell for creamware, and she allowed Wedgwood to rename it Queen's Ware in 1765. Naturally, sales went through the roof. Imitators were quick to follow—potteries in Leeds, Bristol, and Liverpool got into the act by churning out creamware for the masses. Wedgwood went on to triumph after triumph: blue-and-white Jasper Ware; the aptly named drabware; as well as other original styles and patterns still made today not far from the factory where he did his pioneering work.

Today, collectors like Tricia Foley still have a special affection for the oldest and simplest of Wedgwood's designs. Although earlier pieces are more valuable, it's difficult to date creamware due to inconsistent marking practices. As for identifying Wedgwood creamware, look for the name WEDGWOOD printed or impressed on the back of the piece.

all those whites necessarily create a fussy space. Foley has come up with a totally unpretentious, livable look. Part of her secret is her decision to mix her considerable collection of antique creamware, including valuable Wedgwood plates and bowls, with inexpensive contemporary pieces. "If the design is good, the design is good," she says simply.

Years of scouring the markets for that perfect plate have resulted in a diverse collection of old pieces that just keeps growing. On one shopping trip with a friend, she picked up another dozen plates. "He kept saying, 'I can't believe you bought more plates,'" recalls Foley. "He went back to my kitchen and started counting. He said, 'Do you realize you have 120 dinner plates in the kitchen alone?'" But she would rather act now than miss her chance. "When I see something that's really beautifully designed," she says, "I know that I may never see it again."

Foley knows how to edit that passion down as well. Not all those flea market finds are on display—the very best ones are proudly

A SELECTION OF **Foley's creamware picks up the lightly rosy hue of the pine plank floors she had installed in the house. The large bowl with a fluted edge is actually a reproduction of a "Monteith" wine glass cooler made by Mattahedah for Colonial Williamsburg. Most of the other pieces are from the nineteenth century, including a drabware pitcher, a salt-glazed jug, and an artichoke paste teapot by Wedgwood. The cake stands are from Banana Republic.**

shown off in a custom-built rack in the kitchen, so she can see them. "I didn't want to put them all away in closets," she says. Her unfailing eye has created wonderful juxtapositions all over the house, like a stack of 200-year-old plates on a $75 table from Ikea. Instead of calling attention to each other, they get along like old friends, united by color as well as by pared-down style. And this is not a museum where you can look

▶ THE DELICATE DIFFERENCES **among pieces of creamware make for a soothing tableau (opposite). "Instead of a painting, I put my favorite plates on the wall so that I can actually see them," says Foley. "They're works of art themselves." Above: A nineteenth-century footed strawberry rinser (top right), is one of Foley's favorite finds. "I bought it at the Brimfield market in Massachusetts," says Foley of the incised bowl, "and I'm just in love with it." At left is a Dutch basket-weave plate from the mid-1800s that she bought at a London flea market.**

69

FOLEY KEEPS HER EDME PATTERN **dinner service by Wedgwood in plain sight (above), in keeping with the airy and open feeling of the house. Opposite: A stack of pudding and mixing bowls from the early 1900s make for a practical collection indeed—Foley loves to entertain and these help get the party cooking. Next to them is a cider mug from Dorset, England, dating to the 1840s.**

but not touch. "I have no decorative things that I don't use," says Foley.

Above all her other interests is creamware. Though Josiah Wedgwood made it famous, many other manufacturers produced it as well. It became wildly popular in the late eighteenth century, and the appeal has endured—many of the patterns are still made today. "I just love the simplicity and functionality of it," says Foley. "And there's a lot of diversity within that style." Her eye for the very best pieces has been rewarded—

For such a little house, it commands a sweeping view. Located in the hills of Sausalito, California, the shingled cottage owned by Stephen Shubel and Woody Biggs provides the perfect lookout on Richardson Bay—you can even see San Francisco

ROOMService

glimmering away in the distance. Since Shubel is a noted Bay Area interior designer and Biggs is an artist, they had no shortage of aesthetic notions when they bought the house, originally built by a fisherman in 1907. First, they needed to open the place up. "It's an all-redwood house with oak floors,"

a few of them, like a marked Wedgwood plate dating to 1790, are worth serious money. Not that she could part with it at any price. "The edge is crimped, almost as if it were cut from pastry dough with a pinking shear," says Foley with affection. "That's my favorite piece, and the oldest."

She has heightened the effect of her collection with a series of savvy design choices. The white walls of the house enhance the shades of creamware, and the pine plank floor she had installed brings out its lightly buff hue. Seasonal flowers, too, make a great complement. "It's not all white and pure all the time," says Foley. "At Christmas there are big bunches of red tulips, and in the spring, forsythia."

Foley's preference for clean lines reaches its logical conclusion with her collection of lanterns, bottles, and hurricane shades. The shapes are seductive—just look at the old French bottles that conjure up Paris' best bistros—but their transparency allows her chosen palette to rule the roost. Just like the harmonious combination of old and new, it's a delicate balance that works.

▷ **ON THE PORCH, Foley's plates and bowls give way to a collection of glass lanterns, hurricane shades, and bottles. Their transparency is perfect for this transition area of the house—it brings the outside in. Old French bottles—one for olive oil and one for liquor—anchor the table at left. The glass candle cylinder is from Calvin Klein, and the oil lanterns at right date to the 1920s. In the distance is Foley's garden shed, which she added to the original house along with the porch.**

73

says Shubel. "One of the first things we did was paint all the redwood white. It was just too dark for our taste." Except for one chair, almost all the dark wood pieces in the house have been painted, too.

"Since the house is near the water, we wanted lots of nautical touches," says Shubel. The staircase railing, for instance, is a thick length of rope, and the window treatments are white denim, attached with grommets. All these sturdy materials provide balast for lighter, luxurious touches like cashmere throw pillows and gilded mirror frames.

The result is a crisp yet comfortable look. "It's like being on board a boat," says Biggs, though in truth it feels more like a cruise ship than a humble fisherman's craft. Foghorns, seagulls, and the sounds of seals down in the bay add to the effect. Biggs adds, "The house just moves well."

That's true in the sense of the room-to-room progression, but also in the way the design toggles between eras. "It's eclectic, that's for sure," says Shubel. He has mixed fine old antiques with vintage objects in many of the rooms, thereby raising the common design denominator of the whole house.

The color scheme—or lack thereof—is defined by floors that are painted in dramatic black stripes, furniture covered in black-and-white ticking, and clean white walls. The neutral palette dampens any excessive flourishes from the older antiques, and also

▶ **THE COLLECTORS' DOG ROSIE (opposite) looks comfortable on the black-and-white ticking in the living room. The new pressed metal table is Moroccan, but Shubel and Biggs bought it in Paris on one of their frequent visits. The eighteenth-century Italian chair has a gilded edge and represents the rare example of dark wood in the house's interior. Above: A chic black leather tray holds the coffee service, comprised of cups imprinted with selections from a guide to table manners as well as some choice pieces from Biggs' hotel silver collection.**

HOTEL Silver

Hotel guests used to make off with a bathrobe, but today many travelers would prefer to take home the pretty silver coffee pot that decorates their breakfast tray. It's no surprise, then, that collectors comb the Paris and London flea markets for vintage silver trays, toast racks, coffeepots, and flatware used in the grand European hotels at the turn of the twentieth century.

Why the recent surge of interest in vintage hotel silver? The classically simple shapes mix well with contemporary kitchenware as well as with their fussier Tiffany and Gorham cousins—and cost a fraction of the price. While many pieces bear the name of a hotel or ocean liner, the best way to identify vintage hotel silver is its hefty weight. Older pieces were made with special silver-plated nickel to avoid spills on luxury ships and trains, as well as to survive constant use in hotels. They're noticeably heavier than the lightweight silver-plated brass dishes that room service brings today.

provides a backdrop for some of Biggs' artwork. "The black-and-white scheme and the way things are mixed together make it look very contemporary to me," says Shubel. "But if you pick it apart, almost everything is from the nineteenth or early twentieth century."

That mix is the reigning principle in every room: In the bedroom, a French marble-topped end table and gilded, turned-leg stool contrast with a crisply tailored, slipcovered headboard in apple green, the designer's favorite color. "To me, that green is a neutral," says Shubel. It adds a needed punch to black and white, and it brings in the leaf color from trees just outside the window.

Just to make sure things aren't too quietly tasteful, large carved wooden letters hang over the bed, and some are embroidered on pillows. The visual zing of typography provides a focal point and declares Shubel's authorship with S's—in typically eclectic style,

▶ **THE NINETEENTH-CENTURY cabinet came from what Shubel calls "a funky antiques store" in Marin County, and its English Edwardian touches complement the details of the hotel silver. They knew right away it was the perfect vessel for their collection. In addition to the major impact made by all those silvery shapes, the whole display provides an anchor for the room's dining area. The elaborate piece with swan-neck handles on top of the cabinet is an oyster bowl, but Biggs' all-time favorite piece is a humble American cheese cover (above left). It has three holes so the cheese can breathe.**

they even come in different fonts. "I tried to make it whimsical as well," says the designer.

Travel is a major component of these collectors' lives. After several trips to the Loire Valley, they bought themselves a fifteenth-century stone abode there. It has proved a handy home base for frequenting local *brocantes* for offbeat treasures, many of which fit their whimsical sensibility. Their sleuthing has yielded many surprises, including Louis XVI–style chairs, antique oil lamps, and a nineteenth-century priest's robe.

That last item might seem unusual, and it wasn't even bought for a costume collection.

▶ THE RUSTICATED EDGES **of the white bowl filled with starfish (opposite) borrows the look of aged creamware, but it's the only new item in sight. Shubel found the nineteenth-century oil lamp at a flea market in Paris. Above: Though neither the nineteenth-century flatware nor the tray now holding delicate glasses is anything more than silver plated, if polished regularly, says Biggs, they can be the shining star of any table.**

Shubel turned the velvety black robe into slipcovers for pillows and a stool. This isn't just a cheeky move: It shows the knack for abstraction that any good designer must have. A robe's not just a robe, it's a future pillow.

Biggs' own artwork, works on paper depicting urns, are a great tie-in to his 100-piece collection of hotel silver and silverplate,

THE FRENCH ANTIQUE END TABLE (above) marries well with elegant silver toiletries. Right: Shubel's interpretation of European classicism includes a gilded church relic, a nineteenth-century French military cap, and a balloon shade. The addition of Biggs' urn collage is a witty take on the same theme.

replete with urn-shaped champagne buckets and other classical forms and flourishes. "Over the years, we've both gotten very interested in the visual history of Europe," says Biggs.

The silver pieces originally graced the tables of American and European hotels of the last 200 years. As grand as they often are in form—with scallops, garlands, and elegant etching—they were bought for $10 to $20 in most cases. "It had to be durable and inexpensive," says Biggs. "Mostly they used silver plate, but it's a mixture. Sometimes they used nickel, too."

To find these pieces, Biggs adopted disciplined scavenger patterns over a period of seven years. "I had about eight junk stores I went to once a week," he says. "They knew exactly what I wanted, and they would drag it out. You have to go that often, because the good stuff goes fast. And you can't be afraid of a little mold and mildew." The Salvation Army thrift shop doesn't seem like the place to find a relic of the golden age of service, but that's one of the locations Biggs frequented.

That kind of approach has its just rewards. All these character-filled objects fit right in with Shubel's open-minded mix, adding up to a real rarity—the home of a decorator that feels decidedly undecorated. For this iconoclastic pair, the cumulative effect isn't European or American. It's a luxury liner somewhere in-between.

Some collectors are captives to a favorite era, but not Pamela Fritz. The upbeat owner of this San Francisco apartment is attracted to almost anything that has a sense of age, no matter how old. With acute intuition, she uses the textures of gentle fading, light denting,

ELEMENTS
of Alchemy

and layerings of rust and paint for the contribution each can make to her entire home. Like a set designer, Fritz emphasizes the impact of the whole rather than the individual object. The result: echoes of age, hints of color, and fragments of her own past create a

palpable sense of place. Not a real place, mind you, but her ethereal version of eras gone by.

Fritz, a partner in an antiques business, has a typically wandering eye. She searches for, in her own words, "handbags, weird boxes, metal trays, painted metal, old containers." Not to mention other odd objects. It's such a disparate range that a common thread may not seem obvious at

▶ WITH COLORS OF AN INDOOR GARDEN, the muted greens and yellows (left) in this guest room are intended for comfort and invite reflection and refreshment. The furniture includes a potting table now used as a dressing table and a metal garden chair—all chosen because they combine simple, direct shapes with rusticated surfaces. At night, candles lit in the birdcage cast shadows across the white painted floor.

UTILITY Glass

The simple, utilitarian shapes and lucent surfaces of glass storage bottles and jars have become objects of desire for many avid collectors, but to classify all the different types would be an encyclopedic endeavor. Some of the most sought-after pieces are large, hand-blown apothecary jars with remains of labels that identify the original contents. With lids or stoppers intact, apothecary glass can command prices in the $500 range. A much less costly category is the array of smaller bottles designed for health tonics, alcohol, and other liquids. Look for the names of manufacturers embossed on bottles ranging from aqua and cobalt blue to amber.

If you see old bottles in a purplish or rose color, they are often the easiest examples to date. Prior to World War I, manufacturers used manganese dioxide as a chemical agent to clarify glass. Because German blockades prevented shipments of the chemical to reach European glass factories, manufacturers turned to a chemical called selenium which, even after the war ended, continued to be the preferred substance. When glass clarified with manganese dioxide is exposed to sunlight, it turns purple, thus dating that glass to pre–World War I; selenium-treated glass does not produce the same reaction.

first, but there is one: age. Fritzie, as she's called, is obsessed about objects with the type of serious aging that results in crackled paint finishes, distressed patinas, and sometimes even a musty smell. "I love objects that have a story to tell," she says.

Her apartment, a rambling space in a circa 1888 house in the Hayes Valley district of San Francisco, is the perfect setting for a trove of eclectic treasures. Her old industrial ice molds, rusty signs, and funeral vases are all arranged there layer on layer, age on age, overlapping constantly. Sheer organzas and gigantic glass vessels containing spring branches contrast with old walls that have been scraped to reveal decades of past paints and papers. Candles are lit inside birdcages to throw ethereal shadows. While all of these atmospheric enhancers appear to have burst forth spontaneously, they are all part of a carefully conceived plan.

It's no surprise that Fritzie has worked as a photo stylist, a profession based in part on an ability to invent instant visual

▶ LARGE DAME JEAN **jugs filled with spring branches are scattered throughout the apartment because Fritzie loves their rich, voluminous shapes. Dame Jeans are used throughout France to carry wine and other liquids, and they are often found nestled within special wicker hampers. These curvy apothecary bottles, especially prized for their unusual forms, lend a modern air resting atop a rusty garden table.**

narratives. If rooms can be considered giant still lifes, then the alchemy of just the right elements is key to a successful composition. At home, Fritzie changes room schemes often, as much to introduce new "found" objects as to experiment with different background choices.

Living in a house that Fritzie classifies as a constant "work in progress" began when she was growing up on a rather ramshackle Iowa farm. The core of the family home was an 1850s log cabin, which was repeatedly enlarged and surrounded by later remodeling projects, none of which managed to include complete indoor plumbing until the 1980s. In an attempt to impose order on her world, the young Fritzie would "redo" the attic to please her dolls and decorate the barn for the benefit of the chickens, always using whatever objects were at hand.

"I'd use what I could find," she says. "Doorknobs, old bottles, and hangers— it wasn't bad training. It helped to develop the idea of making do, making sense, and giving order. The mind-set was similar to what I do today, when I've got a beautiful

▶ SAP BUCKETS IN IMPRESSIONIST COLORS line the dining room wall, seen in the mirror's reflection. They change into giant candelabrum at night, when pillar candles are lit within, and the whole room glows. Canning jars, another symbol of cottage industry, are filled with poppies and create a bright color field. Aqua glass was the most commonly used for disposable storage prior to World War I, after which clear glass became the standard.

IN A SITTING ROOM (opposite), the distressed finish on two 1920s industrial ice molds filled with olive branches seems to reiterate the room's wall finish, which was created with repeated applications of paint remover. The modern 1960s bench—with its black leather cushion and shiny chrome frame—acts as a visual relief to the complicated textures nearby. Above: The aqua tint of a glass mold is just the right complement to the magnolia blossoms it contains.

old door, but have to figure out what else it can be. A tabletop?"

Adaptive reuse seems to be Fritzie's calling card. Since 1996, she has been a partner in Interieurs Perdu, an antiques store that stocks old farm tables, metal cabinets, funeral and religious artifacts, and wrought iron—all characterized by a cast-off air and heavy distressing. The store's devoted clientele knows it's the place for a look of decayed elegance and "rescued" objects.

Today, one of Fritzie's prized collections is her grouping of signs depicting numbers. With a bold, graphic appeal, they come from various industries; some are old printing letters and others are commercial signs, such as numbers from old gas stations. Fritzie uses them in her study, mounting them on the walls like art. Many come from flea markets and antiques shops in Iowa, still a favorite hunting ground during trips home to see her family.

"The signs are bright, colorful, and sort of shocking," she says. "They always look fresh." When arranging her objects around her home, Fritzie combines them with colors and textures as an ensemble. She tends to start with pale shades that are almost white, but then she adds a touch of color like mocha or sage green. Then she leaves a lot of space around the objects so they can breathe, and so they make visual sense.

Fritzie doesn't pretend that her affection for each piece of junk—and that's what most of it is—makes rational sense. Her intuition about placement and combination, however, has turned it into something else. Like a weekend alchemist surrounded by apothecary bottles full of homemade potions, she has turned junk into *junque*.

▶ BRIGHTLY COLORED POPPIES **(opposite and above) are arranged in wooden containers that have been stamped with printing numbers from the owner's collection. Overleaf: In the study, a trio of French green metal office chairs line up alongside a worktable that serves as a desk. As color wheel opposites, the red of the numbered signs pops against the room's vivid green paint.**

It sounds like a decorating riddle: "It's old and white, and goes with anything." What's Gretchen Mann talking about? Ironstone, of course. Mann is a collector who has socked away some 600 pieces of ironstone in her white clapboard house, built around 1820

DRAWN to Scale

near lovely Old Lyme, Connecticut. But she doesn't like the white stuff for its virginal impeccability— rather, she fancies its casual accessibility. "It looks good against white walls, or any kind of walls for that matter," she says. "And it's very functional. I have stacks of it everywhere, and I use it." Ironstone does

not require an antique pedestal in Mann's everyday scheme. "Originally, it was the Woolworth's of china," she says. In fact, she likes when it shows its considerable age. "The older it gets, the cracklier it gets," she says. "It gets veins in it, and character."

Mann, a designer by profession who is quite a character herself, has been buying ironstone for about ten years—a period during which it's become incredibly popular. "It's so hot now, and there are so many books on it, that it's getting scarcer," she says. Still, her perseverance has paid off. Mann is not one of those people who goes out looking for ironstone. Rather, she looks for ironstone whenever she happens to go out.

This constant scrounging leads her to buy in bulk if possible—and only at the less fancy antiques shops and flea markets. No auctions, no high-end dealers. Her rule of thumb: "If a platter is around $40 or less, the prices are good there." Small shops in Dorset, Vermont, and Westerly, Rhode Island, have been particularly fruitful, and she doesn't mind venturing into a place that looks "crummy," since that's where the good bargains are. If she's buying ironstone for a design client, she'll purchase it in large numbers and siphon off the unusual pieces for herself.

Mann gives beginning collectors some standard advice—"Buy what you like"—as well as some unheard-of advice—"Buy for

▶ THE TABLE IN THE **dining room (opposite) could comfortably seat twelve, and its surface is painted with a delicate scallop motif, taken right from the library of classical design details used in ironstone patterns. Mann's tureens and pitchers often take center stage, as their architectural forms echo the finial collection and the house itself. The restaurant chairs, probably Italian ones dating to the 1930s, sport a covering of—get this—vinyl. "It's the new leather," jokes Mann. Above: In another view of the room, you can see that old garden baskets have been employed for holding wine and fruit. Mann likes white so much that she spray painted the Spanish chandelier herself.**

WHITE Ironstone

Unpretentious and purist, plain white ironstone was the classic Gap T-shirt of nineteenth-century china. English Staffordshire potters created ironstone for American and European middle-class families who demanded dishes that didn't break. The sturdy stoneware earned its name from the traces of powdered iron rumored to be included in the patented porcelain look-alike.

The ironstone style drew predominately on a mix of Asian and European influences. Europeans favored eccentric Chinese-inspired patterns that were anything but plain—they were dressed up with dragons, rose medallions, and exotic floral designs. But the shapes of the china, especially pitchers and tureens, were unmistakably English Georgian in style. Hare's head handles, curls, bulges, and frills of the rococo revival reminded the upper classes of the porcelain their forefathers accumulated throughout the eighteenth century.

Americans liked the architectural forms but preferred them patternless, thank you very much. Housewives concerned with hygiene believed that plain white plates were easier to clean, and sets of pristine ironstone were snapped up by the thousands. They knew that just like today's classic T-shirt, you can never have too many.

quantity, not quality," she says. "That makes much more of a statement with ironstone. More is better." It's not that Mann wants you to end up with lackluster plates. She just figures you can sift through them later.

Among its many charms, ironstone provides one of the strong notes of white in Mann's sharply focused world of color. "Everything in the house is black and white, or gray and white," she says, appropriately wearing a black-and-white checked suit (with a red scarf as an accent.)

She's exaggerating for effect, of course—there are naïve paintings of cows in the kitchen with green grass showing, and leopard-print fabrics in a number of places. But then again, exaggerating for effect is the point of Mann's whole decorating scheme.

Connecticut interiors have a reputation for being uptight, "decorated" spaces, and the Mann household is anything but. After all, Mann and her husband, Mowry,

▶ INSTALLING A RACK **on the back of a door—and then placing an ironstone platter inside (top left)—is typical of Mann's unflashy ingenuity. Opposite: The house dates to the 1820s, and the scalloped niche corner cupboard is part of the original architecture. Instead of appearing starkly white, the ironstone assortment actually takes on the shade of the rest of the room. "The walls are a taupy, mocha color," says Mann, "which gives it a nice cast. At night it's great in there—it's like a dark little bistro."**

live on a ten-acre property that includes a menagerie of seventy-five animals—including ten dogs, four hourses, a donkey, a lama, and thirty chickens. (Luckily there's also a barn.) Since everyone has to spread out, Mann says her guiding design principles are, "Big and open, but sparse. Everything huge."

The huge criterion is filled by her other main passion, architectural finials—yes, those large, usually wooden forms found on top of barns, at the bottom of banisters, and all over architecture from the nineteenth century. "I don't like a lot of

IRONSTONE AND **nineteenth-century iron compotes (opposite) both inhabit an American slant-back cupboard, circa 1790, that is topped with a weather vane from 1810. The diamond pattern of the floor leads the eye right to the cupboard, and this high-key contrast provides an unexpected sense of visual surprise to the hallway. The 1820s gilded English mirror adds a glossy touch to this black-and-white scheme. Above: A stand that used to support an aquarium now holds an assortment that includes turtle shells in an ironstone tureen and a rare, heart-shaped iron finial from the eighteenth century.**

little stuff hanging around," says Mann. "If you're going to dust things, dust big."

Many of these ball-shaped pieces are from the period 1820 to 1840, when they started gussying up New England farms. Not

107

ARCHITECTURAL Finials

Peeling paint and weathered wood have always been a reality with farmhouse owners, but only on the outside. Antique architectural elements—finials, columns, and pedestals that once decorated the doorways, gardens, and rooftops of English country manors, Italian palazzos, and Greek Revival houses across New England—are the gems of the architectural salvage world. And they're being brought indoors.

Their sculptural shapes lend "architectural bones" to even the most featureless room, and well-worn patinas contribute a unique sense of texture that's hard to find anywhere else. As with antique furniture, collectors vie for pieces with provenance. Neoclassical designs from England and Italy are favored, and the materials of choice are marble, bronze, and zinc, since they last longer than wood. Among woods, hardwoods like mahogany and cherry fare better than pine. If you favor finials, pairs have the highest value.

coincidentally, the house dates to the same era. "I don't care where they come from, as long as they come," Mann claims, but she has naturally honed in on this same period for many of her design choices.

Standing all together on a table in her living room, the finials produce an Alice-in-Wonderland effect: They look like outsized chess pieces. Ironically, the scale and stature of the modest room are enhanced, not diminished, by their presence.

Though the strong shapes of the finials are attractive, the texture is also crucial—their rough surfaces, weathered by the elements, throw a patina of age over everything. What Mann calls their "old chippy paint" also plays off the gracefully aging ironstone: They're growing old together. Appropriately enough for a house near Old Lyme, heritage and history have never seemed so alive.

▷ **MANN'S all-time favorite finial is this French example (left), made from French oak and topped with a gilded pineapple. It was also her most expensive: two of them cost $2,000, since they're more expensive in pairs. Opposite: A variety of woods show their "old chippy paint." According to Mann, "mahogany, cherry, and oak are desirable, because they last. Zinc is great because it never goes bad. Anything made with pine or the softer woods is usually rotten." In this grouping most are oak and cherry—except the biggest, which is made from pine and is showing its age. Mann placed them all on a pine table from the late nineteenth century, which she whitewashed herself.**

If you'd like to know the next big thing in collecting twentieth-century design, you might want to ask Sara Blumberg and James Oliveira. They're only in their mid-thirties, but the instincts of this dynamic duo have proved prescient so far. "For years we had setups of 1950s and

LEARNING Curves

1960s glass ceramics at the 26th Street Flea Market," recalls James. "No one knew what to make of us. Slowly we got people into it, and the people who sell it now were our customers then." These days, midcentury baubles like the ones they sold are hot indeed. It's not that these art dealers are necessarily smarter than you and

me—they've developed their instincts and have learned to tune out the white noise of the market. "We're interested in pedigree, but we're also interested in pure design," says Sara. That could be a boast, but they back it up by both collecting for themselves (and dealing in) $100 objects as well as $1,000 ones. If they like it, they like it.

And the real proof comes in the couple's 5,000-square-foot loft in Jaffrey, New Hampshire. Though they keep a small apartment in New York City, their New England home represents the epitome of their taste.

▶ **A KNOLL SOFA** and colorful blanket mimic the strong horizontal lines of the former candlepin bowling alley in Sara and Jim's New Hampshire loft. One of the 1950s pedestal tables holds a gourdlike work by the Andersen Studio (seen also on page 113 with others by the Maine-based couple). The shelves are full of the couple's studio pottery finds from around the world—most are Andersen pieces, with a few Danish works thrown in. The orange and red Scandinavian chargers are actually plastic, and Jim has given them a Jackson Pollock touch by personalizing them with ink and acrylic paint.

115

STUDIO Pottery

The clean lines, sophisticated textures, and infinite array of colors of twentieth-century American studio pottery are a far cry from the humble designs of their clay ancestors. Whether the subtle objects of Scandinavian origin, or the more exuberant American versions, modern studio pottery by artists like Wilhem Käge, Edwin and Mary Scheier, and Gertrud and Otto Natzler consistently challenges the style books and scientific formulas of art pottery.

Responsible for changes good and bad in architecture and design during the eighteenth and nineteenth centuries, the Industrial Revolution changed the manufacturing process of pottery for good. New factories spat out thousands of pieces of pottery per day—their goal to stock the kitchens and dining rooms of middle-class Europe and America quickly and inexpensively.

The Scandinavians were the first to rebel. They began to address the need for "good design for everyday use" around 1916. For Swedish artist and alchemist Wilhem Käge, this meant inventing hundreds of new glazes.

The Americans were quick to follow suit, benefiting from the influx of European designers during the 1930s and 1940s. The Scheiers were a husband-wife team famous for creating slightly off-center pieces. Also thumbing their noses at machine-made perfection were Weston and Brenda Andersen of East Boothbay Maine (many of their pieces are seen on this spread).

The recent boom of interest in twentieth-century studio pottery from Sweden, Denmark, Germany, and Italy will soon be catching up to their equally unique American counterparts.

It exudes a fun, full-blooded modernism—not the more severe kind.

"We're constantly revolving the pieces," says James, and there are plenty of beautifully designed objects to choose from. After all, Jim started collecting at the precocious age of ten, when his hometown of Enfield, Connecticut, started digging up the town as part of an urban renewal project. "I started to find old bottles, and then I was collecting them," he says. "It's an instinct."

Appropriately enough, the couple met while working at a Manhattan art gallery. Then nine years ago, a friend asked them to unload a bunch of antiques. So they decided to set up a booth at the flea market. In one

▶ A LEATHER AND WOOD CHAIR in the style of Danish designer Jens Risom (opposite) has a remarkably similar line to a table that Jim and Sara believe to be by Frank Lloyd Wright from the 1950s. The table holds a pair of cased glass vases made in Italy in the 1960s. Above: A row of what Jim calls "purely aesthetic pieces" includes three midcentury wooden bottles from (left to right) Norway, West Germany, and America. A piece of American outsider art from the 1930s evinces Jim's passion for the human figure. A piece of Italian cased glass from the 1960s blends in, based on color, one of the galvanizing principles of the loft's design.

of their first weekends they came across a piece of Czech glass from the 1920s. "We were intrigued by it and did some research," says Jim. "That's how we got into art glass. After that it was a natural evolution."

Italian glass is one of the fields that now consumes them, particularly the stunning

A GROUP OF MORE PEDIGREED **Italian glass** includes a bottle designed by Gianfranco Purisol for IVR Mazzega in 1961, which stands to the left of a piece designed by Anselo Fuga for AVEM in the mid-1950s. Above right: An incised bottle made by the Venini company from the same era. Paolo Venini, the founder of Venini, designed the decanter (opposite) for his own company in 1956. All of these pieces are worth $1,000–$3,000.

shapes that have been produced for hundreds of years on the fabled isle of Murano in the Venetian lagoon. They've also been buying American studio pottery from the 1950s to the 1980s, especially the simple bowls and vases made by Weston and Brenda Andersen in East Boothbay, Maine. Not to mention twentieth-century Scandinavian pottery.

What do these disparate fields have in common? Looking at the pottery shapes on display, you can see how the crosscurrents of design have flowed from Europe to America and back. But Sara has a more elemental reason: "It all comes down to form." In relating why they love one group of Andersen pieces, she calls them "organic," and the same could be said about all their favorite objects—not to mention the way they've decorated their home.

Their loft was a former candlepin bowling alley, and Sara and Jim have not tried to fight the strong lines of the wood

floors or regular pattern of the exposed brick walls. Furniture from the 1950s—some pedigreed, some not—anchors the look. In the living room area, a sleek Knoll sofa looks square (in a good way) under some colorful, round Scandinavian chargers that Jim has painted with his abstract expressionist take on the female form. For dining, there's a Smith College library table from the same era that they bought at auction.

Their biggest achievement has been to embrace bold color, which is a lot easier since all the objects themselves have a crisp shape. "All this 1950s stuff is pretty clean-lined,"

MURANO Glass

Although it looks thoroughly modern, the twentieth-century Murano art glass is firmly rooted in the past. In fact, the grandfathers of the glass industry in Europe, the glassmakers of ancient Rome, would feel right at home on the tiny Venetian island of Murano today.

Since the year 1291, when the government voted to move all the glass furnaces to Murano to protect the city of Venice from fire, the island has been the epicenter of Italian glasswork. Due to the success of the high-quality, colorful plates, vases, and decanters they produced, Murano glassmakers continued to use the same multistep techniques to blow handmade glass through the centuries.

Jump to the year 1921, when an entrepreneurial Milanese lawyer named Paolo Venini founded a new glassworks in Murano with the help of Venetian antiques dealer Giacomo Cappellin. Venini did the unthinkable and hired a painter, Vittorio Zecchin, to design a new, modern style of Murano glass. Venini then paid the master craftsmen of Murano to make glass according to Zecchin's new designs.

The craftsmen must have been skeptical when Zecchin presented them with simple, monochromatic designs with the clean lines and classic proportions of Renaissance and ancient Roman glass.

Venini's company became a roaring success, and he continued to push the envelope, hiring sculptors (Napoleon Martinuzzi), and later architects (Carlo Scarpa and Tommaso Buzzi), to design glass throughout the 1930s, 1940s and 1950s. Of course, the competition also rushed to institute the new collaboration between craftsman and designer—the result being the thousands of innovative designs produced in Murano throughout the twentieth century.

says Sara. "Even if one element is over the top—like the color—it doesn't take over."

The sofa sports a positively prismatic wool blanket that they didn't even buy—it just got delivered with the sofa because Sara was overheard praising it in the shop. That kind of serendipity occurs because of their total commitment to aesthetics. "I paint, and we both do some writing," says Jim. "That's our whole lifestyle, and collecting is a part of it."

▶ **FLUVIO BIANCONI'S "fasci verticale" bowls for Venini (opposite) are a much cheaper form of Murano, which can sometimes be found for as little as $150. Above: A library table from Smith College and a set of Heywood-Wakefield school chairs, all from the 1950s, set a learned tone for the Renaissance couple. The table is topped by a selection of European art glass. The two tall vases at left are Tapio Wirkkala's designs for Venini circa 1966, and at far right is a Wirkkala design in amethyst glass for the German company Rosenthal.**

You don't think of wing chairs, 150-year-old oil portraits, and delicately decorated transferware as the building blocks of an uncluttered look. Somehow, antiques dealer Ginger Ludacer makes this contradiction work in her Greenport, Long Island home.

BENDING the Rules

Everything she owns has personality—and you have a chance to grasp the reasons why, since each one is given substantial breathing room. You can almost see the objects that were placed and then removed, leaving only the best examples behind. She certainly comes across plenty of quality material in her day job:

she and her husband, Ken, run the trend-setting Beall & Bell antiques shop in Greenport, where magazine editors are known to shop in search of the latest look.

Despite her eight years of professional experience, Ludacer doesn't think of herself as a collector—except when necessary. "It's good to say that you collect something, that way your family knows what to get you as a present," she says, laughing. "Most of my transferware plates were given to me by my mother."

Ludacer now owns about twenty of these beautiful old plates. But like everything else in her house—shared with Ken and their young son, Thomas—what she's done with them is counterintuitive and clever. Instead of displaying them in the kitchen or dining room, many of them are upstairs in a guest bedroom, mounted on the wall above a bed right next to some scarlet-and-white toile de Jouy curtains. "It's the most popular guest room," she says.

The bucolic scenes are echoed ingeniously downstairs in the living room. Ludacer covered a wing chair in blue-and-white toile, and the Asian fantasy depicted there, replete

▶ **DANISH CHAIRS meet American pottery in the Ludacer kitchen. Arne Jacobsen's plywood chair design, circa 1955, has modern curves that are unexpectedly echoed in the artichokelike pattern on green bowls made by the venerable McCoy company of Roseville, Ohio. The bow of the table's iron legs adds to the curvy chorus. The slab marble top was added to the table when the Ludacers customized and expanded it.**

WIREWARE

The tinker played a very real role in European life during the seventeenth, eighteenth, and nineteenth centuries. In Slovakia, tinkers traveled the countryside from farm to farm, stopping to mend broken pottery and precious glass jars using thin laminated wire. Wire quickly became a coveted craft throughout Europe and America, as it proved to be durable, inexpensive, and easily bent into household necessities.

At the turn of the nineteenth century, the Industrial Revolution swept through European kitchens and dining rooms, replacing wire with more durable enamel and stainless steel. The most resourceful tinkers responded by creating stunningly sophisticated decorative wire objects.

Soon every bride-to-be wanted a wire trousseau basket, and wedding guests often showered newlyweds with wirework fruit stands, candelabras, and chandeliers. Wire especially suited the gadget-minded; hinged baskets that transformed from cake stand to lettuce dryer were sought after by novelty hunters and cooks alike.

Wireware's prosaic past is all but forgotten when looked upon today: its airy designs transcend new heights, recalling the fanciful wire sculptures of Alexander Calder or the elegant drawings of Saul Steinberg.

▶ LUDACER'S great-great-grandparents, featured in the nineteenth-century oil paintings (above), preside over an Art Deco mirrored sideboard from the 1930s that is topped by a humble wireware basket and some family crystal. Opposite: Ludacer sought out Plexicraft's Lucite table since she knew it would balance the room's old-fashioned chairs. In the back left corner, an Empire-style sewing table holds a mercury glass lamp as well as a whimsical silver and lucite candlestick by Dorothea Thorpe. The sofa is a copy of a Jean-Michel Frank 1930s design. As for rugs here, no thanks. "It would seem too fussy, and I like the original pine floors," says Ludacer.

with sailing ships and birds, isn't inappropriate for Greenport. Located at the far east end of Long Island, it's a small village on the North Fork, a world away, psychologically at least, from the trendy Hamptons on the South Fork.

Two years ago, the Ludacers bought (for a song) their gracious house, a ten-room affair built in the 1880s. It's a block and a half from their shop. "I'm from New Orleans, and the inside of the house felt like a New Orleans house to me," says Ludacer. "The mouldings, the mantle—there's a touch of formality. It's not a farmhouse."

So when they conceived of how they would live, the Ludacers didn't fight that formality. And they had a trump card: a wonderful family inheritance far better than money. "A lot of the furniture we have is my grandmother's," says Ginger. "It came out of her Spanish-style house in New Orleans."

But true to form, Ludacer knew how to pare back even this meaningful legacy— she didn't keep everything. "My grandmother probably had ten chairs in her living room, and we have three," she says. "She had three sofas, we have one. I don't like a lot of stuff. We deal with that all day long at the shop."

The sentimental attachment to some of the pieces also solves a typical problem for antiques dealers, who often rotate their home decor as they buy and sell their inventory. "Because so many of the pieces are my grandmother's, we won't ever sell them,"

she says. "It's nice to know that these things will always be there."

Ludacer's eye for mixing styles and eras—"We're kind of all over the map," she admits—is instinctual and assured. In the living room, ornate Victorian armchairs (reupholstered since grandma had them) sit across from a funky, 1960s Lucite table, as does the toiled wing chair. In addition to being useful, the rectangular clear table serves to clear the way through the room, allowing visitors to visually take in the more substantial pieces in all their glory.

It's a vision typical of Ludacer's open-minded approach. "It's too confining to have just one thing," she says, explaining her reluctance to amass lots of particular collections. Instead of building up her stock of transferware, Ludacer mixes it with green McCoy bowls and wireware baskets. "It would feel like a museum and not a real house," she adds. "You have to be able to buy something that strikes you, no matter what it is."

▶ **THE TOILE CURTAINS were bought at the Brimfield antiques market, and Ludacer thought that mounted transferware would amplify the pastoral scenes. The plates create graphic symmetry all on their own, and from far away they come across as pure texture and color. They're mounted above an American sleigh bed from the 1920s. An old silver-plated trophy makes a home for hydrangeas that emphasize the room's seductive and unusual palette, and a sisal rug doesn't distract from this colorful scene.**

TRANSFERWARE

A dressed-up version of English creamware, transferware is named for the process by which a simple cream-colored plate, pot, or vase procures its pattern.

Around 1756, potters developed a process for pressing a thin piece of damp tissue to an inked copper plate; then they pressed the tissue onto the china, thus transferring the pattern. Whimsical scenes of pagodas, gardens, or beautiful ladies transformed a plain-Jane plate into chic crockery.

Transferware was most popular during the first half of the nineteenth century because the society set could replace broken pieces in their costly collections of Chinese porcelain with the blue and white look-alikes—without their dinner guests being the wiser. The middle classes loved transferware because they could finally afford to own the fashionable blue-and-white china.

Pastoral scenes of grazing animals and bucolic landscapes soon joined the Asian-style designs as favorite patterns.

Today, blue transferware is still considered most desirable, thus commanding higher prices than its red (very rare), brown, black, purple, and green younger cousins.

In the land of sailboat pictures and hunt prints that is the Connecticut suburbs, Susan Crandell's house makes a striking first impression. The white Victorian-era house, built in 1886, looks conventional enough from the outside. But if you peer through one of

MENDING Fences

the many tall windows, you'll see what a lifetime of intelligent art and artifact collecting can do to a plain white interior. "When we moved out of the city twenty-one years ago," says Crandell, "we had been collecting lots of large canvases. The natural daylight and high ceilings were perfect for us." So she and her husband,

Bob, immediately installed works by masters like Susan Rothenberg and Richard Diebenkorn, and have added many more over the years. They have an impressive collection of contemporary abstract and figural works they've been amassing for almost thirty years.

Crandell, a historic preservationist by trade, also appreciated the fact that her new

▶ A DARK PAINTING by Louisa Chase (left) complements the room's other dramatic shapes. The architectural elements in the window include a pleasing diversity of materials. At the far ends are two wooden finials that came from newel posts. The larger iron finials came from New England and date to the nineteenth century. "They're big and heavy, and the dealer was probably happy to sell them," jokes Crandell, who picked them up at the Wilton antiques show for $200. The mercury glass globe stands on a wooden capital.

135

house was in a true neighborhood of other, similar houses instead of the spaced-out far suburbs. The old adage goes that good fences make good neighbors, and Crandell has a nice one of her own that surrounds the elegant home. She has also put her own unique spin on the idea: Most of her fences are *inside* the house.

For six years, Crandell has been collecting fence finials. "I like them because they're wonderful shapes that look terrific against pale-colored walls," she says of the mostly iron fragments. "And they're architectural, which is meaningful to me." The bold, black shapes are unusual, and they work on two levels: as an abstract design element and as a sober, proper remnant of history. A pretty neat trick.

She has about sixteen of these fragments, and they come in some truly amazing shapes. "Some of them even have a provenance," says Crandell. Six finely wrought roses that came from a circa-1860 fence in Ohio adorn one mantlepiece in the dining room. "I first bought two and adored them," she says. "But I realized they would look even better as a large set, so I called the dealer and he sent six more."

Each one cost close to $200—as Crandell puts it, "None of this stuff is cheap." But considering the visual impact, they seem like a bargain, especially when placed under valuable artworks that cost a

▷ CHILDREN'S CHAIRS **(opposite) are among Crandell's smaller collections. Made of wood and wicker, they date to the nineteenth and early twentieth century and now fit snugly under a wooden shelf that she had treated with silver leafing. A sea-grass rug emphasizes the fairly casual look. "I'm always trying to get things to be less formal," says Crandell. Above: The star-shaped leaves that once belonged to a fence are showing their age, but the collector doesn't mind—the patina makes them even more alluring. "I don't do anything to them," she says. "Some are rusting, some aren't."**

137

hundred times more. But it took Crandell a while to figure out how to fine-tune the display of these diverse collections.

"The last time I decorated—before this current scheme—it was much brighter," says Crandell. "There was much more color, but I felt it was fighting with all the elements I'm really interested in. So this time around, I tried to smooth it all out."

White walls are the first building block, as they are for many collectors. "For the art, you've got to keep things as simple as possible," says Crandell. Celadon green furniture provides the subtlest hint of color, and it wasn't chosen at random. The thistles, roses, and long spiky leaves depicted in the iron fragments all allude to another passion of Crandell's: gardening. Her plot of perennials and shade-loving plants can be seen in back of the house.

To bring the outside in, Crandell maximizes the use of her windowsills, so often ignored or used as a throw-pillow zone. In one, she has interspersed four finials and two

▶ **THE MOST ELABORATE finial in Crandell's collection has to be the thistle, trefoil, and star combination that may have once separated a proper garden from a lawn. Fresh-cut flowers help emphasize the details and bring the piece to life. Above the mantel—like the moldings, it is part of the house's original equipment—is an untitled charcoal drawing by Susan Rothenberg, one of several works by the artist on display.**

IRON Fragments

It's recycling that doesn't involve bottles and cans: designers, architects, and flea market connoisseurs search for iron artifacts salvaged from estates and the exteriors of old buildings. Bringing cast-off metal ornament (including wrought-iron gates, posts, grates, and railings) indoors pays homage to the artistic detail of a once-flourishing craft.

While some salvage-seekers transform grates into coffee tables or window guards into wall decor, garden gate fragments often bear a floral motif and stand on their own as decorative objects. Iron artifact enthusiasts scour salvage yards and shops specializing in architectural elements for remnants that range in price from $25 to many thousands of dollars.

If you're lucky enough to stumble across a piece of ornate, spiraled iron stair railing bent and twisted into shape by French Art Deco blacksmith Edgar Brandt (who signed every piece E. Brandt), act quickly—one panel of his balcony railing is worth as much as $5,000.

A ROW OF CHINESE **export porcelain (above) follows the line of an antique dining-room table. Running perpendicular along a mantel are the six individual roses that once graced a fence in Ohio. "Apparently, the fence itself was very plain," says Crandell, "but these finials are just unbelievable." The Susan Rothenberg work above is called *Black Struts*. Opposite: The scrolling lines of an Empire sofa from the mid-nineteenth century create a comfortable interior backdrop for finials that used to weather the elements.**

slim topiaries; these mini-trees recreate the original habitat of the fragments. The mercury glass globe in the center adds to the row's stately profile. A dark Alexander Calder mobile drifts above this assemblage, further encouraging the eye to reduce the room's contents to their fascinating outlines.

To the side is a wooden ladder from the Philippines, one of several ladders Crandell owns, and it echoes the vertical lines of the objects on the windowsill. It also reintroduces the hand of the artist. The imperfect curves of each step were carved with the same attention that went into the brushstrokes of Crandell's art collection.

It's a measure of Crandell's assurance that she can add traditional Chinese export porcelain to this tableau and make it seem unstodgy. "The blue-and-white is wonderfully fresh," she says of a series of nineteenth-century ginger jars on the dining room table. "My mother collected it, and I've always loved it. I use it a lot."

But she doesn't dote on them the way she does the finials. Crandell has three children, and the maternal instinct can be heard in the way she talks about her fence fragments. "You have to really love them, and they need space to breath," she says. As for why she has followed her instincts down this particularly fertile garden path, that's easy. "You have to be willing to take a risk," she says. "Who wants to be like everybody else?"

THE COLLECTOR'S EYE

When I was five, my mother took me to a shop that belonged to a friend of a relative in my hometown of San Francisco. It was filled with old furniture and dusty objects, and I remember a certain desk globe that intrigued me most. In such a big world, anything seemed possible.

LIGHT and Aerie

Perhaps that's why I moved east to New York, the capital of vintage design. I remember that wonderful blank-slate feeling when we moved into our home several years ago. My husband, Keith Scott Morton, and I were the second owners of a prewar apartment that badly needed reinvention. We didn't really own much furniture or, rather,

furniture that we wanted to keep. Keith's work in photography makes him attuned to light, so we started with what we knew. In those first few days, watching the eastern-facing rooms fill with sun made it easy to see that only pale washes of color on the walls would do.

We started with an overhaul of the kitchen, an impossibly cramped museum of 1950s Kenmore appliances that led to an enormous porcelain double sink positioned awkwardly at the back of the room. There were even swinging doors—obviously not a cook's kitchen, a suspicion later confirmed by neighbors who knew the previous tenants. Our architect had come up with a plan that we loved. It was Cubist in attitude, but still

JUST OUTSIDE the kitchen's windows (opposite), planters were placed at the same height as the work islands, lending a leafy view onto the terrace. Above the islands hang shelves of glass and metal pipe that imitate Wright's materials and keep a collection of the crystal glassware within easy reach. The platters mounted on the back wall, designed of spun aluminum by Wright, serve as visual balance to the room's many angles. Above: Three pieces from Russel Wright's early designs in spun aluminum include a cylindrical pitcher with a twisted wooden handle, a ball pitcher with a rattan-wrapped handle, and a ladle.

sensitive to the old world building. The plain white tiles used in 1927 were replaced with the same type, and the glass tile floor border reminded us of the New York City subway murals that date back to the 1930s.

It was my small but growing collection of Russel Wright glassware and aluminum pieces that ended up inspiring many of our

147

A GROUP OF **crystal water tumblers, pilsners, and assorted stemware (above) glow with the soft tints of seafoam, coral, and chartreuse, three of Wright's most popular colors. Opposite: The kitchen's dining banquette is actually a birch veneer bench pulled up to a milk glass–topped metal table. The niche displays a small group of Dansk metal pitchers, and the pendant lights mimic upside-down wine glasses. The table is set for a buffet with a variety of turquoise platters from Steubenville and Glidden.**

material choices and paint colors. The glass and steel shelving we installed above the work islands was an ideal perch for the glassware. The vegetable-tinted tones of the crystal, from Wright's American Modern collection, would be illuminated by soft but steady northern light. From a practical standpoint, their earthy colors and elegant forms pulled together all my other mismatched tableware.

When we entertain, I love to mix it all up according to season or mood. With limited cupboard space, the new rule was that every object we collected had to work hard and look good at the same time. Russel Wright would have approved, summing it up nicely in the title of his postwar primer, *Guide to Easier Living*. Plus, it was an affordable (guilt-free) choice that still satisfied my addiction to shopping for vintage whenever I could.

Even if on-line auctions have forever changed the way people shop—I'm fascinated by it, and the hours evaporate whenever I browse—I'm still a hands-on person. The best part about frequenting shows was getting to know the terrific dealers that supplied us

RUSSEL Wright

Often dubbed the first American industrial designer, Russel Wright caused a stir in the New York design community when he started to sell products evoking the sleek lines and no-nonsense attitude of modern European design. Predicated on the idea of creating good design for the masses, his vision of a new and casual lifestyle for America was enthusiastically embraced.

Wright may be known best for the "coupe" (rimless) plate design and earthy colors of his American Modern Dinnerware that grossed over $150 million for Steubenville Pottery from 1939 to 1959. But his early spun aluminum, chrome, and pewter teakettles, coffeepots, and cooking utensils won him fame at the beginning of his career. The utilitarian pieces were snapped up by consumers who prized their exquisite handcrafting. Wright signed all his metal objects, but they're hard to come by today and command high prices.

Easier to find, and less expensive, are examples of Wright's colored glassware in natural hues. Originally designed to complement his American Modern dinnerware, the stems and tumblers, manufactured by Old Morgantown, are the essence of versatility.

with much of our furniture, housewares, and decorative objects. Through that experience, I learned to ignore distractions and look for the simple forms that attract my eye. I'll go to great lengths to acquire just the right piece; I've shipped plates from Miami and dragged crystal pieces (along with a pair of andirons) back from Prague.

That's not to say my instincts are infallible. What about the French recamier I bought that was too short for a twentieth-century body? It didn't fit in its intended place in the bedroom, either. It took a while to learn how to walk away from a seductive object, content to know that it would've been a great buy if we had a twenty-room house to decorate.

Instead, we filled our living room with small, easy-to-move-around vintage furniture and a large, comfortable sofa. Benches double as tables and dining chairs multitask as desk chairs. The room has a masculine

THE TABLE SETTING'S simplicity (previous pages) gets enhanced by a sophisticated color palette—a Steubenville salad bowl in bean brown, a dark green pitcher by Iroquois, an amethyst Tapio Wirkkala water carafe, and lots of mercury glass and silver. Wedgwood Drab dinnerware heightens the effect of the clean white salad plates that were designed by Wright for Steubenville. Vintage Puiforcat flatware, found at a local thrift store, offsets the splurge on crystal water glasses by Moser. Right: The living room's furnishings include a few tag sale treasures. The 1930s plaster barley twist lamp was bought for $75, and the 1950s "X" benches were rescued when the building's lobby was redecorated. The dining chairs were designed by Gilbert Rohde for Herman Miller in the 1930s. Sheer blue linen curtain fabric and rattan shades from Windoware help to filter out the city.

air—one of the few patterns on display is the wool pinstripe on the throw pillows.

Our main collection is a group of green glass from Empoli, Italy, some of which is presumed to have been designed by Gio Ponti. It was love at first sight—to me, glass lends lightness to a room, and these forms were streamlined and classical. They produce the same effect that greenery does: a burst of vibrant color that's versatile enough to go in any setting. The collection inspired a soft, yellow-green for the walls (it was hand-mixed and probably can't be duplicated, so don't try this at home). The taupes and natural tones lend cohesiveness and a restful quality, despite the presence of our daughter Natasha's toys and other household debris that settles in the room.

You won't see a lot of art on these walls. It doesn't mean we don't love it, but this room seemed fully occupied already. After a long process of adding and subtracting, we've finally come up with a crisp practicality that we're really happy looking at every day. We wouldn't change a thing— at least not until next week, that is.

▶ A COLLECTION OF 1930S and 1940s hand-blown green glass from Empoli, Italy, brings a welcome note of clear color to the room's neutral palette. This type of glass has roots in the Tuscan tradition of utilitarian flasks and tableware, but with one important distinction: The sensuous forms seen here resulted from the artistic movement that brought Italy's famous architects and designers together with Empoli's glass-works. These are presumed to have been designed by Gio Ponti.

155

Resource Guide

BOOKS

Baroview, Marino, Susanne K. Frantz, and Lino Tagliapietra. *Venetian Glass*. New York: Charta, 2001.

Barr, Sheldon and John Bigelow Taylor. *Venetian Glass: Confections in Glass: 1855–1914*. New York: Harry N. Abrams, 1998.

Williams, Petra. *Staffordshire Romantic Transfer Patterns*. vols. I, II, and III. Fountain House East.

Godden, Geoffrey A. *Encyclopedia of British Pottery and Porcelain Marks*. Barrie & Jenkins, 1991.

Coysh, A.W. and R.K. Henrywood. *The Dictionary of Blue and White Printed Pottery 1780–1880*. vols. I and II. Suffolk: The Antique Collectors' Club, 1982 and 1989.

Creswick, Alice. *The Fruit Jar Works*. vols. I and II. N. Muskegon: Douglas M. Laybourne, 1995.

Kerr, Ann. *Russel Wright*. Paducah, Ky: Collector Books, 1997.

Keller, Joe and Daniel Ross. *Russel Wright*. New York: Schiffer Publishing Ltd., 2000.

Wetherbee, Jean. *White Ironstone: A Collector's Guide*. Antique Trader Books, 1996.

Roberts, Gaye Blake. *Mason's: The First Two Hundred Years*. London: Merrell Holberton, 1996.

Godden, Geoffrey. *Mason's China and the Ironstone Wares*. Suffolk: Antique Collectors' Club, revised edition, 1993.

Slessin, Suzanne, Daniel Rozensztroch, Jean-Louis Menard, Stafford Cliff, and Gilles De Chabaneix. *Wire*. New York: Abbeville Press, 1994.

Kahr, Joan. *Edgar Brandt: Master of Art Deco Ironwork*. New York: Harry N. Abrams, 1999.

Schiffer, Herbert. *Antique Iron*. New York: Schiffer Publishing Ltd., 1999.

Pina, Leslie. *Designed and Signed: 50's and 60's Glass, Ceramic and Metalware*. New York: Schiffer Publishing Ltd., 1999.

Swingle, Daniel and Dale R. Stoin. *Burley Winter: An Introduction*. 1999.

Watson, Oliver and Ian Thomas. *Studio Pottery*. San Francisco: Chronicle Books, 1993.

Riddick, Sarah and Richard Green. *Pioneer Studio Pottery: The Milner-White Collection*. The Antique Collector's Club, 1991.

Pina, Leslie, Donald Johnson, and Brian Higgins. *Adventures in Glass*. New York: Schiffer Publishing Ltd.

NEWSLETTERS AND ORGANIZATIONS

The Modernism Magazine
(609) 397-4104
www.ragoarts.com

Vetri: Italian Glass News
www.vetri-italianglassnews.com
P.O. Box 191
Fort Lee, NJ 07024
(201) 969-0373

The Midwest Fruit Jar and Bottle Club
Norman Barnet
P.O. Box 38
Muncie, IN 47308
(812) 587-5560
www.fruitjar.org

Midwest Fruit Jar and Bottle Club Shows
Horizon Convention Center
401 S. High Street
Muncie, IN 47305
(812) 587-5560

Wedgwood Collectors Society
P.O. Box 14013
Newark, NY 07198

White Ironstone Notes/WICA
Box 536
Redding Ridge, CT 06876
www.whiteironstonechina.com

Transferware Collector's Club
1113 Alexander Drive
Augusta, GA 30909
(706) 733-7743

WEBSITES

www.ebay.com

www.transcollectorsclub.com

www.Icon20.com

www.worldcollectorsnet.com/-wedgwood

www.antiquebottles.com

www.kovels.com

Eppraisals.com

www.auctions-on-line.com

www.manitoga.org
(For information on guided tours of the house Russel Wright designed for his family on the Hudson River in New York. His daughter still lives there and the house contains many of his original designs.)

ANTIQUE SHOWS AND FLEA MARKET SOURCE INFORMATION

The Official Directory of U.S. Flea Markets
New York: Ballantine Books, 2000
(800) 733-3000

The Newtown Bee
P.O. Box 5503
Newtown, CT 06470
(203) 426-3141
www.thebee.com
(For subscriptions and other information)

www.stellashows.com

www.wendyantiquesshows.com

Sanford Smith Associates
(212) 777-5218

DEALERS IN SPECIALTY ITEMS

Wireware
American Primitive Gallery
594 Broadway, Room 205
New York, NY 10012
(212) 966-1530

Kathryn Berenson Quilts
7206 Meadow Lane
Chevy Chase, MD 20815
(301) 718-0570

Ironstone and Transferware
The Bucks County Antiques
Center/Lisa Worden
(215) 794-9180

The White Ironstone
Association
P.O. Box 855
Fairport, NY 14450-0855
(For further information)

Architectural Elements
Architectural Antique
Exchange
715 N. Second Street
Philadelphia, PA 10123
(215) 922-3669

Urban Archaeology
143 Franklin Street
New York, NY 10013
(212) 431-4646

Tobin Townsend
Box 22
Callicoon Center, NY 12724
jet@catskill.net

Iron Artifacts
Architectural Artifacts, Inc.
4325 North Ravenswood
Chicago, IL 60613
(312) 348-0622

ADMAC
111 Saranac Street
Littleton, NH 03561
(603) 444-1200

Associated Building
Wreckers
352 Albany Street
Springfield, MA 01105
(800) 448-2822

United House Wrecking
535 Hope Street
Stamford, CT 06906
(203) 348-5371

**Russel Wright and Other
Midcentury Designers**
William K. Straus
Upstairs Downtown
12 West 19th Street
New York, NY 10011
(212) 989-8715

**Italian Glass and Other
Midcentury Glass**
Glass Past
(212) 343-2524

A & J 20th Century Designs
255 Lafayette Street
New York, NY 10012
(212) 226-6290

Mondo Cane
143 West 22nd Street
New York, NY 10011
(646) 486-7616

Cosmo
314 Wythe Avenue
Brooklyn, NY 11211
(718) 302-4662

**McCoy and Other
Commercial Art Wares**
M.E. Collins
c/o The Showplace
40 West 25th Street
New York, NY 10011
(212) 627-9609

David Stypmann Co.
190 Sixth Avenue
New York, NY 10013
(212) 226-5717

**Studio Pottery and
Decorative Arts**
(Arts and Crafts)
The Perrault Rago Gallery
17 South Main Street
Lambertville, PA 08530
(609) 397-9374

Ark Antiques
P.O. Box 3133
New Haven, CT 06515
(203) 498-8572

**Studio Pottery and
Furniture**
Lin Weinberg
84 Wooster Street
New York, NY 10012
(212) 219-3022

Vintage Looks
Interieur Perdu
340 Bryant Street
San Francisco, CA 94107
(415) 543-1616

Hunters & Collectors
P.O. Box 1932
Bridgehampton, NY 11932
(631) 537-4233

Beall & Bell
18 South Street
Greenport, NY 11944
(631) 477-8239

America
Five South Main Street
Lambertville, NJ 08530
(609) 397-6966

Ruby Beets Antiques
1703 Montauk Highway
Bridgehampton, NY 11932
(631) 537-2802

SUPPLIERS

page 8:
**Alexandria Display Cubes/
Exposures**
(800) 222-4947 (to order)

pages 38 and 40:
**Aalto Dining Chair and
Sofa Fabrics**
Larsen Fabrics—Cowtan
and Tout
(212) 647-6900

page 42:
Sheer Linen Curtain Fabric
Pollack Associates
(212) 627-7766

Curtain Trim
Fortuny, Inc.
(212) 753-7153

pages 150–151:
**Drabware Dinnerware/
Waterford Wedgwood**
(800) 677-7860

pages 152–153:
Nakura Natural Roman Shade
Windoware by Smith & Noble
Call (800) 765-7776 for a
catalog

**Pinstripe Wool Fabric on
Sofa Pillows**
Holland & Sherry Inc.
(212) 758-5373

**"Lino" Sheer Blue
Linen Fabric**
JAB—Stroheim & Romann
(718) 706-7000

Gilbert Rohde Dining Chairs
William Doyle Galleries
175 East 87th Street
New York, NY 10128
(212) 427-2730

1930s Armchair
Paterae Soho
458 Broome Street
New York, NY 10013
(212) 941-0880

Armchair/Custom Leather
Hermes Leather
45 West 34th Street
New York, NY 10001
(212) 947-1151

Furniture Refinishing
Rafael's Furniture
Restoration
655 Atlantic Street
Stamford, CT 06902
(203) 358-3079

Fabrication
Sew and Sew
165 West 4th Street
New York, NY 10014

DESIGNERS

pages 36–49:
Design Fabrication
Christine Churchill and
Natasha Bergreen
Interiors Haberdashery
737 Canal Street
Stamford, CT 06902

page 146:
Claus Rademacher Architects
(212) 535-1800

James Scott Weaver AIA
532 Madison Avenue, 6th fl.
New York, NY 10019

Morrie Breger
(609) 397-7090

Stephen Shubel Designs
P. O. Box 0960
Ross, CA 94957

Gretchen Mann Designs
Lyme, CT. 06371

Tricia Foley
1388 Lexington Avenue
New York, NY 10128

157

ACKNOWLEDGMENTS

Thanks go to my wonderful husband, Keith, who turned vision into reality; to our Natasha, for knowing patience beyond her two years; to my talented teammates, co-writer Ted Loos and designer Susi Oberhelman for so seamlessly connecting their own creativity to the project; to my editors at HarperCollins, Megan Newman and Edwin Tan, whose steadfast enthusiasm and good humor saw us through, to Ann Cahn for her brilliant production editing, and to Karen Lumley for her production expertise; to Eliza Alsop, Mitchell Owens, Scott Weaver, Melissa Sellars, Judy Naftulin, George Waffle, Tom Dolle, Trish Foley, Nancy Soriano, Randy Bourne, Debra Deboise, and Ted Jones for each of their invaluable roles; to my mother Natalie, to my sister Kay and brother Bryan for the true constant of their love and support; and to Paula O'Shea and W. Scott and Phyllis Morton for insightful advice when it was needed most; to Sally for all the indispensable help at home and to Ellen and Lily, fantastic friends and neighbors; and finally, to the extraordinary energy of Bill Straus, Sara Blumberg, and Jim Oliveira, whose dedication to their trade was in equal measure to the time and expertise they shared with me—and to Gary Lin and Larry Weinberg, who, along with many other dealers, foster an American tradition of great design.

Index